T0090487

WAKE ME UP AT 10:00 LOVE, TERRY

FRANCES S. FERGUSON

BALBOA.PRESS
A DIVISION OF HAY HOUSE

Balboa Press books may be ordered through booksellers or by contacting:

Balboa Press
A Division of Hay House
1663 Liberty Drive
Bloomington, IN 47403
www.balboapress.com
844-682-1282

Print information available on the last page.

ISBN: 979-8-7652-3405-1 (sc)
ISBN: 979-8-7652-3407-5 (hc)
ISBN: 979-8-7652-3406-8 (e)

Library of Congress Control Number: 2022916135

Balboa Press rev. date: 09/24/2022

Contents

PART ONE

PART TWO

PART THREE

Dedication

Blessed are those who mourn, for they shall be comforted.

Introduction

In the spring of 1984, Christopher Bernard Wilder, a serial killer, was on a killing spree across the United States. He tortured, raped, and murdered eleven beautiful young women. He was shot to death in Colebrook, New Hampshire, April 13th of the same year, trying to escape into Canada. My twenty-one- year-old daughter, Terry, was his first confirmed victim.

Getting to know me … this is who I am

"An inextinguishable laughter shakes the skies." That's what is written under my yearbook picture. Guess I laughed a lot, but I can't remember that far back. Another thing written about me was, "Her loyalty to her close friends cannot be equaled." So now you know I was and am, funny and, I was, and still am, loyal. I am funny. I have a wicked sense of humor I was born with that trails me like a relentless shadow. My mental chatter accompanies my day-to-day life. You know, the voice in your head that never stops. The voice in my head thinks it's "on stage" 90% of the time because it's always shooting out "one-liners." This voice has little if any respect for what's right or wrong. It just spews its opinions out whenever it wants to, and, as I said, that's 90% of the time. What happens to the remaining 10%, I'll never know. *I remember I've always had funny things happen to me. Like right now, I am writing something and everything is slanted. Why? Who is doing this funny thing? Are funny things happening to me because I think they always do? Are there just funny things that happen to me? Only the shadow knows.*

I see things differently and find humor everywhere because I believe everything has a touch of humor attached. Whatever it is, if you look a little deeper, you will discover it. It's like the frosting on the cake, a rainbow after the storm. Sometimes it's so very light it can barely be seen; other times, it's really piled on and can't be missed. It's an entity of its own.

Another thing to know about me is I'm an animal lover, all animals, great and small. If you're unkind to any animal, you will never be a friend of mine. It's that simple. I'm the person who stops traffic on a busy road to let a turtle get to the other side or any critter, for that matter. That's part of who I am.

At one time, I was an avid golfer and a good one. It seems I have a natural ability for it and am competitive by nature. I have one hell of a golf swing. My favorite part of the game is chipping, getting as close to the pin as possible to make putting easier. You know the drill, keep your head down, follow-through, don't peek, blah, blah, blah, then miss the damn putt. I loved the game, though, and played three or four times a week "back in the day." It was all about focus. First, you would picture where you wanted your ball to go, believe it would, and you would play the result of your belief. You had to imagine what you wanted very clearly. Life is like the game of golf, isn't it? Know what you want, believe you can have it, then do all it takes to follow through to your goal. Golf is a game you play against yourself. At least it was for me. If I parred a hole one time, I'd try for a birdie the next time (one less stroke). Add three more golfing friends to the mix, and it was always a blast.

Gardening is one of my many joys, from digging in the dirt to planning and planting all the flowers I can squeeze into my garden. It's challenging to go to a garden center and not come back with much more than my list called for and somehow manage to fit them in with their other friends. My mom used to say, "it's not a full garden until all the flowers are touching hands." In my garden, they don't have far to reach.

Added to the mix is art. Since I was a little girl, I have loved to draw. As I grew older, I learned how to paint and to appreciate the artists from centuries ago. My favorite painters were the Impressionists. They saw beyond the obvious colors and painted what they felt, so all their works seemed to vibrate. Seeing beyond the obvious in your everyday life has its benefits too.

I have many other passions. My main passion is to help others who have lost a child. My heart aches with theirs because I've crossed that bridge, the one that breaks hearts. I'm on the other side now because of my own daughter's death, with knowledge, hope, and love to share to ease that awful pain. Unless you have walked in the shoes of those grieving the loss of a child, you just don't know, or ever will know, what their lives are like. I do. And I want to be the person to help others cross that bridge when they are ready.

Although I cry easily, they are not always tears of sorrow. They are tears of joy, beauty, and gratefulness of what I am a part of. There has never been any parade that doesn't find me choking back tears. The sound of Taps played at a military funeral or our flag flying by touches my soul and brings appreciation for all those who selflessly sacrificed their own lives for ours. But it's the loss of a loved one and the pain I see reflected in their eyes; that is the reason why I wrote this book.

Now that you know something about me, I want to share with you the events in my life that touched my soul and changed who I am today.

Here is my story.

Now when I sweep the floor of your room,
I sweep not dust, nor crumbs.
I sweep your footsteps every one.
Happy footsteps trudging in
From golden beaches, blazing sun,
Heavy footsteps slowed now from work,
Joyous footsteps, still dancing from the night,
But footsteps of your life I sweep, and
With every movement of the broom I weep,
For no more footsteps shall I sweep.
-F.F.- 1984

City of
Indian Harbour Beach Police Departmen

Chief of Police
F. Ferrai

August 6, 1985

Detective Godffrey Shelley
New South Wales State Police
Austrailia

Dear Detective Shelley,

You and I have never met, nor in all probability will we, yet I have an important request to make of you. I am personally having difficulty with my own local and federal government in getting information on Christopher Bernard Wilder's past. Was he an American with a passport to Austrailia, an Austrailian with a passport to the United States, or was he both? I cannot find out.

Could you, without jeapordizing or violating your country's security or regulations, pass on this information and any other information you might have to me? I will, of course, reimburse you any fee for reports or copies entailed.

If you are curious as to why I write, it is not as a fellow law enforcement officer, it is because I had a bright, funny, beautiful twenty-one year old daughter whom I loved with my whole heart. She was Wilder's first confirmed victim. Nothing will bring her back and my insides will live with this hurt until I die, but now there is a desparate need to know more about the man himself. Could you help?

Yours truly,

Capt. Donald H. Ferguson

DHF/kdh

The letter

I held a copy of his letter in my hands, a letter written a year after my daughter was murdered, and slowly absorbed the truth as each word seeped into my heart with pain, remorse and understanding.

It was a letter written decades ago by my husband. A letter that would have changed our lives had I read it sooner, though it was never, ever meant to have been read until now.

No one will ever know or will they understand the impact this letter from decades ago, had on my heart. The words simply have not yet been created. Softly tracing his signature with my fingertips at the end of the letter, I longed to touch his heart, to ease the pain it silently held secret.

He had loved her and I never thought he did. When she was killed, I cried alone. I grieved alone. All because I thought, in grief, I was alone.

Now I see his words written on a piece of paper that says I was wrong. We both grieved separately and silently and because of this, we parted.

Terry

Child, I miss you, friend of mine.
How I'd love, just one more time
To sit and talk and laugh awhile, and
Catch the moment in your smile
And hold it close while we're apart.
Oh child, my child, you took my heart.

St. Theresa's Prayer

May today there be peace within. May you trust God that you are exactly where you are meant to be.

May you not forget the infinite possibilities that are born of faith.

May you use those gifts that you have received and pass on the love that has been given to you.

May you be content knowing you are a child of God. Let this presence settle into your bones and allow your soul the freedom to sing, dance, praise and love.

It is there for each and every one of us.

Part One

CHAPTER ONE

MY LIFE SHATTERED INTO MILLIONS of pieces when my daughter was killed. If you have had the same experience of losing a child or a loved one, you know how I felt and what I went through. We become related.

Life was pretty ordinary until it suddenly ended up in fragments at my feet. To lose someone you love brings tidal waves of emotions, and those waves of emotions affect everyone surrounding you. Unfortunately, those same waves can drag you into depths of despair and drown you in sorrow forever if someone doesn't throw you a lifeline.

My lifeline showed up as an extraordinary woman who became, and still is, my lifeline to knowledge, joy and hope. With this story, the same experience, joy, and hope become my gift to you.

1984

The typewriter switch is on, but I just sit here looking around at her half-repainted bedroom walls. Her Raggedy Ann and two other favorite stuffed toys still wedge themselves by her pillow, seemingly waiting for her return, and my heart wonders how to start when I can't even see what I'm writing through the tears. Just how do I begin to tell a love story that is older than the sea?

* * *

On the eastern seaboard, slightly south of the midsection of Florida, spring unraveled from winter. The shrimp still dallied in the Indian and Banana Rivers, eluding the last hopeful fishermen lining the banks and bridges nightly with long-handled nets and lanterns. Beaches were spotted with snowbirds in their pink-white plumage while native youngsters still wore their wet suits surfing to keep off the water's chill. Area citrus trees bore the last burnished gold and orange shades of fruit, swaying lazily whenever a rare breeze blows.

Florida's Space Coast was enjoying the weather it was famous for. To the south, West Palm Beach and Fort Lauderdale were filling with college students on spring break, and eighty miles north, Daytona Beach handled the overflow. Offering little excitement for college students, the small city of Satellite Beach was well satisfied with its location.

Only a four and a half hours away in the Miami area a monster had begun his trail of horror. Christopher Bernard Wilder, a thirty-nine-year-old businessman, had gone over the edge and was moving north, leaving two beautiful young women missing in his wake. One whom he had dated and asked to marry. Later, police would theorize that it was this woman's rejection of his marriage proposal that catapulted him over the precipice to madness. A repeat sex offender with a record dating back to 1962 in his home of Australia, Wilder was a walking time bomb. The fuse had been lit. He was now heading for the one who would become his first confirmed victim, my twenty-one-year- old daughter, Terry.

Wilder led police and the FBI on one of the most intensive manhunts in the nation's history, leaving at least twelve women from Florida to California shot, knifed, sexually molested, strangled, or mutilated. Three survived. Four are still missing. All occurring from the end of February 1984 until April 13 of the same year when he killed himself in a struggle with police at the Canadian border in New Hampshire.

* * *

"Mum, how come your eyelashes are so short and stubby?"

There she was again, her face reflecting beside mine in the bathroom mirror. It seemed whenever I went in to put on makeup, invariably, there she would be, overseeing my attempts at self-improvement. Within a few minutes, by some very subtle body moves on her part, she would be in front of the mirror, and I would be trying to squeeze in to finish what I had started. The mirror would reflect her beautiful face with big brown doe eyes surrounded by thick black eyelashes, one of her best features. They looked woefully innocent but danced with secrets. She hated her full lips, so she rarely wore lipstick.

Her nose was straight with a slight upward tilt at the end. Every one of her features enhanced the others. Her shoulder-length hair was dark brown and became flecked with red and gold when struck by the sunlight, a perfect frame for her picture-pretty face. I knew Terry's reflection completely hid her lack of self-esteem. She told me many times that she never felt smart enough or pretty enough compared to others. To some, she appeared offish, even snobbish, but those few who knew her well knew she was merely camouflaging all her insecurities. At five foot seven and 115 pounds, with perfect measurements, she would always turn heads, men and women alike. When she and I would go shopping together at the mall, walking from one store to another, I used to kid her and say how nice I felt having all those young men stare at me. I told her not to feel slighted, that someday she, too, would be attractive and maybe they would look at her. Terry would flash me a grin and we'd keep on walking.

It was on these shopping expeditions of ours that she would pull her favorite trick, which really ticked me off to put it mildly because it would embarrass me so. She would drop behind me about fifteen yards or so in the parking lot or down the mall's central aisle. She would then pretend to be blind as a bat, and with arms flailing in front of her or groping all around, she'd yell to me, "Mom, please, Mom, wait for me. I know you're ashamed that I'm blind, but I can't help it. Please wait for me. I'll try to keep up. I'm sorry!"

People, of course, would turn and stare, first at her then questionably at me. Terry loved that one, and how she kept a straight face through the whole thing I don't know. The more I raised my voice telling her to cut it out, the more she implored me for forgiveness. I wanted to wither into the pavement.

Her friends knew better than anyone that fun was a large part of her life. They all have their own memories of her that I feel sure bring smiles to their lips.

One I can vividly picture that she told me about happened

a few years ago. She and her girlfriend, a Southern Baptist and a born-again Christian, decided to check out one of those adult bookstores where they have dirty movies to watch in little booths. She never told me of plans like these in advance, of course, but I would hear of such little adventures afterward. She would preface these conversations with, "Mum, promise you won't get mad if I tell you something."

She and her friend watched one of the movies and satisfied their curiosity, but when they went to open the door and leave, the door jammed. Her friend panicked, not from claustrophobia but from the thought that the door might have to be opened by the fire department and maybe even the police. If this happened, her parents would find out, and they'd kill her for being in this kind of a place. The harder her friend tugged on the door with a look of desperation, the harder Terry roared with laughter. Finally, her friend could take no more and started crying. By then, tears were coming down Terry's face too, but they were tears much different from those of her friend. Terry was not laughing at her friend but at the situation itself, which was so hilarious. By the time the manager heard them and finally came and opened the door, they both fell out, one weak from laughter, the other from fear.

As if she had to squeeze so much living into so little space, Terry was always in a state of rushing. If there was something she had to do or somewhere she had to go, she always seemed to thrive on running late and swearing like a trooper when she couldn't find her car keys at the last minute. She would routinely look high and low for her keys then tear out the door to her car. Her car, a red and white 1977 Pontiac Sunbird, was another part of her. How it had survived God only knows. There was a leak in the radiator that she "couldn't find time to have fixed," so she carried two gallons of water in plastic milk jugs on the floor of the back seat and topped off the radiator with the garden hose almost every day before leaving for work.

Once, she had a leak in the gas tank too, so I crawled under the car and fixed it with stuff I bought at a service station. It worked, but her gas tank never saw a full tank anyway. She fed her gas tank two or three dollars' worth at a time, and for some unknown reason, she never ran out! Looking back, I believe I know where that leak may have been born. A few minutes after leaving for work one afternoon, she came into the house and hopelessly slumped into the living room chair by the front door. Tears of frustration puddled in her eyes, giving them the appearance of moist chocolates.

"This is just great; the engine just fell out of my car!"

I thought, *Why do all these calamities always happen when the husband is at work? How soon could it be fixed?* These questions flew through my mind as well as the fact she would be late for work unless I drove her right now.

"Oh, Terry, how could it? Engines just don't fall out of cars, do they? Let's go out and take a look."

We went out to examine the problem (talk about the blind leading the blind). It didn't take a detective or a mechanic to spot the problem. She had run over our metal garbage can, and it was securely wedged between the road and the car. I got down on my back, placed my feet on the bumper, and pulled it out slowly. I still shake my head when I think of that episode. She drove off to work with a wave and a," Thanks, ma!"

Why is it these little things endeared her so to me? The girl's car must have had a guardian angel.

Many other things went wrong with that poor car. She had to have it towed so many times that her insurance company finally canceled her towing insurance. A bald tire meant little to her, and if her father hadn't kept putting new ones on, she would scarcely have neither cared nor noticed.

Her car took her from point A to point B. How it did so was no concern of hers. It only mattered if, for some reason, it didn't. She had no idea how it ran or why.

On the floor of the car's passenger side was all the junk she didn't take time to throw out daily. There were empty Wendy's and McDonald's wrappers, candy bar wrappers, a few empty beer cans, many empty Tab cans, crumbled papers, beach thongs, a few old socks, and usually over a half dozen of our drinking glasses from the house, which she would use to drink her Tab. Once every couple of months, she would take some sort of pity on it and empty it. It would stay clean for only a day or two at the most, no more. Then the whole process would begin again. Her car usually had the look of a party in progress or at least a small-scale picnic.

Her room bore the exact resemblance. In the evening, when she left on a date or left with her girlfriends to go dancing at the local Holiday Inn, she was impeccable, not a hair out of place. She could grace the cover of any magazine with her artful makeup and love of fashion. Unfortunately, her room was in absolute shambles with powder and makeup all over her bureau and desk. On the floor, clothes that were tried on settled in little rejected heaps where Terry discarded them for other choices. The small sign in her room said it all. "Please don't straighten out the mess in my room … you'll confuse me and screw up my whole world."

After many battles of "Make your bed, pick up your room," she found a "Condemned "sign and hung it on the outside of her bedroom door. The door remained shut. This may not have been the solution to some, but it was for us. What we didn't see didn't bother us.

There were many times I would look at her when she was not aware of it and wonder what she was really like, this beautiful child of mine, deep down inside, the part that was hers alone. Oh, I knew the surface personality; what mother doesn't know what her daughter likes or dislikes? Terry had excellent taste in everything, and it showed in her clothes, jewelry, and places she frequented.

A hard worker, she began her first part-time job when she was fifteen. She never saved money. It went for school clothes, after-school hamburgers, movies, and junk. She never asked for nor expected much that she couldn't supply herself. Terry was much more conscientious at work than she was with anything she had to do around the house. If she had ever asked if she could help me with the housework, I probably would have fainted.

One of her proudest achievements was being asked to join the local college fraternity, which she did. She had her little Phi Beta Kappa card but never filled it out nor carried it in her wallet. Instead, she stuffed it into her jewelry box where it still remains.

Few, if any of her friends, knew of the poems she would write, some troubled and some touching; her lovely verses are hidden away on little scraps of paper, shared with no one. I found one on her bed one day and commented on how good it was. She seemed surprised. Although she desperately wanted to be someone special, she shunned her talents and the praise that would come from the very things she excelled in.

We were unalike in many ways, but our love for one another was the perfect weld.

CHAPTER TWO

MARCH 18, 1984, HER NOTE read, "Mum, wake me up at 10:00, Love, Terry."

It was one of the countless notes and added bits of communication so familiar to both of us; notes on the refrigerator were left by me for her if we did not see each other coming and going during the day. Notes on the bathroom mirror were posted for her when she came in after a date, and we had gone to bed, telling her who called and their message; notes, notes, notes, never a note without some kind of humor in it, we both loved to laugh and shared a rare type of humor.

There were nights she would wake me laughing over a note I had left her because I never left a straight message. Whatever the message, I would doctor it up to ridiculous proportions. If someone unknown to me called, I would still add something to the note, such as "good old Brad called and will call tomorrow. By the way, how are his parents" I've been concerned about them, Did his dog, Ralph die? Give him my best, Love, Mum". Sometimes I would leave a note telling her that someone called, and I told them that she thought they were ugly creeps and wished they would never call again.

Her notes to me were equally funny. It was nothing to come home and find on the refrigerator a note reading, "Howdy folks, I have gone out to a wild sex orgy, have no idea when I'll be back, depends on how long the drugs hold out, Love, Terry." I wish now I had kept some of her masterpieces that had me laughing until I cried. I still have her last note, which would be the beginning of every parent's nightmare and a horror story that the nation and the world would eventually know.

The end of her life, heartbreaking as it was, was not an end at all but a beginning. As she was always giving to her family and her friends, it should not surprise them to receive this, her last gift, the most precious of any she could provide, meant to last their lifetime, the gift of love and the knowledge of life everlasting, and more, so much more.

That bright sunny morning in March, my mother was visiting from Massachusetts. Terry and I sat in the backyard eating tangerines off the tree and getting some sun. Terry was in a tranquil mood - kind of "offish." She wasn't her usual happy self. I thought maybe it was because she had been out late the night before with her girlfriends or because she had bumped into her old boyfriend who was with another girl and that it had bothered her. For whatever reason, she seemed moody, so I left her alone. Mom and Terry were comparing foot sizes of all things and were surprised to find they both had the same narrow heel and wore identical shoe sizes.

The sun was too hot for me. I went into the house,

fiddling with things in the kitchen, looking up from time to time, watching the two of them. Terry wanted to look her best that night because her boyfriend, Dan, was coming back from spring break in Fort Lauderdale with his best friend. Dan and Terry had been dating for almost two years now. After a painful breakup with a previous boyfriend with whom she had been very much in love, she had met Dan.

When she started talking about him a lot at home, I knew we'd be meeting him soon. They hadn't dated yet, just met, talked, and danced when they went out with their respective friends. Then Dan breezed through the front door with Terry one day while I was in the kitchen paring vegetables for dinner. Although Terry had told me all about him and how gorgeous he was, I didn't expect anyone could match her description. Dan did not. He excelled. We shook hands while I stood by the sink; his appearance struck me suddenly as funny, only because I never saw someone quite so perfectly handsome. Where were the young men like this hiding when I was young?

Talking easily with me and grinning at Terry from time to time, I saw two, what I would call "make-believe" people standing there like two perfect Barbie and Ken dolls. Dan, in just his swim trunks, his 6'2" tanned body showing time spent working out at the nearby gym, his blond hair carefully styled, blue/green eyes shining, and a smile, dentists work for. Side by side, Terry and Dan balanced the scale of beauty.

"Hey, that's weird," Dan exclaimed. "My mom has the same poem on her refrigerator as you do on yours, and it's just as old and yellow."

I looked up from the sink to the verse "Footprints" and thought, "Dan, I like your mom already."

The plans for the night of March 18th were that Dan and Terry were to double date with one of her co-workers and Dan's best friend. Dan had called Terry the night before from a telephone booth while a line of impatient callers waited their turn. As Terry talked, he reminded her of the others waiting for the phone. Finally, he told her he had to go, and that is when Terry implored him to stay on the line, saying, "Dan, wait, there's something very important I have to tell you."

Dan was puzzled with what she said, not so much by its meaning but by its urgency. Her words to him were, "Dan, remember, as long as you live, no one will love you as much as I do." Those were to be the last words she would ever speak to him.

About noon, she came into the house through the Florida room to the dining room, standing briefly in front of the large oval mirror, checking how her tan was coming along. She had enough, went into the bathroom to shower, and then left the house wearing my pink blouse over a tank top, her favorite Calvin Klein's, and comfortable boots. Terry and I wore the same size blouse, so she often wore my sweaters, jackets, and blouses. Terry would already have been in my closet, selected what she wanted, put it on, then would come to me and ask, "Hey Mum, is it okay if I wear this?" I always said yes, but my only request was to return it as clean as when she borrowed it. She was not good at this, and whatever she borrowed eventually made it as far as the hamper, and I took it from there. Knowing this in advance, I always had the option of flat refusal. I never did. Things like that just didn't get me upset or angry. I remembered being that young with a mind that was going in every direction at once. She said goodbye to us all, and that funny feeling hit me in the pit of my stomach as she walked quickly out the door, down the driveway to her car.

Terry headed for the Merritt Island shopping mall to buy something special to wear that night. She was to meet a girlfriend first, and they were to go shopping together. She got into her car, waved to my mother, who was standing by the front door watching, and drove away.

That was the last time we saw my daughter.

What happened at the mall, we'll never really know. We learned later, Christopher Wilder had been in the area on and off for years. We know that he had photographed girls Terry knew from high school in local pageants in the county. We have heard this man was charming, good-looking, and well dressed. We know now, he was a mad killer. If he had approached her and asked her to come to his car to show her pictures of her friends, mentioning them by name, or just having her sign a modeling contract, would she have gone? It would seem relatively harmless to her in broad daylight to do something like that. We know she would not have voluntarily gone with him in his car. She was not gullible, and being a policeman's daughter, she knew what could happen at any time. She would also be in a hurry to get home for her date. It took her a long time to get ready. I knew she would be home at 3:00 or 3:30 PM at the latest. She wasn't.

Between 3:00 and 8:00 PM, Terry was dead.

Terry was luckier than most of Wilder's victims. She was not sexually assaulted or tortured. Instead, he beat her severely, breaking her ribs and rupturing her spleen, savagely kicking her with his boots. We know she fought like a tiger. Her 115 pounds were no match for his maniacal fury. I will forever fight thoughts of Terry's last struggle and paralyzing fear.

She was hogtied with a rope, her mouth duct-taped. Terry was then thrown into the trunk of his car, driven to a deserted orange grove where she cheated Wilder out of whatever more he had in store for her by strangling herself trying to get free. Ironically, Wilders' convertible got stuck in an old orange grove a few minutes drive from the mall, and Wilder had to go to a nearby house and call a wrecker to tow him out. All the time, Terry was in the trunk. I wonder if this was when she died, trying desperately to free herself, to shout to the voices she could hear? I'll never know.

All parents, at times, have premonitions or feelings of foreboding, sensations of something about to go wrong. I was no different. So many other times when Terry went out that door, I would get those "gut feelings." I never had a reason for it or didn't think I did. I would worry, though, until she pulled up in front of the house again, safe and sound. This was another of those times; I dismissed it and went on doing the everyday things I usually do around the house.

Dan called when he and his friend got back from Ft. Lauderdale and was surprised Terry wasn't home yet. So was I. After 3:30 PM, I kept roaming to the front window watching for her car to pull up. It was now 5:30 PM, and something was wrong. My husband Don, a Captain with the Indian Harbour Beach Police Department, said we were worrying over nothing. She would be home soon. When 6:30 PM came, Dan called again and wondered if she had been mad at him for going to Ft. Lauderdale, angry enough to stand him up. It was a definite possibility.

At the time, I thought it was because she just couldn't stand the thought of him going there without her. She was very insecure and jealous and feared Dan might meet or date another girl, devastating her.

I am a believer in God and prayer. I was praying in my mind on and off and was rambling from room to room, having short conversations with mom, who was doing the same. About 8:00 PM, I had a feeling inside that everything was okay … a definite sense of peace came over me, putting my worry aside momentarily. (I was to learn much later that this was when she died.) Besides, Terry had stopped first to pick up a friend so they could go shopping together.

Knowing the two girls were with each other seemed proof that she was indeed mad at Dan and was "fixing" him, as she used to say.

It grew dark before I remembered this particular friend had no telephone, but why didn't Terry find a payphone? She could be mad at Dan but would never do this to me. Never. We were best friends. Could they have gone to a party, come back, and fallen asleep? That had to be it. She had never failed to call me when she was due home and couldn't make it on time. By this time, mom was a wreck. Fortunately, my dad had already flown home a few days earlier and was unaware of any problem. How we all got through the night with one ear listening for the front door, the other for the telephone, I don't remember. The porch light burned all night, waiting with us.

But she never called.

My husband, Don, went into work the following day, neither of us saying much. We were baffled at this point. Surely, she would come flying in the door any second, apologizing and telling the wildest story, but she didn't. After Don was at work, he left for the T-shirt printing factory where Terry worked as quality control supervisor. She was supposed to be on the morning shift. She just had to be there! But Terry was not.

It was Monday, 8:00 AM when Terry's boyfriends' little yellow Austin Healy wheeled into the driveway, and Dan hurried into our living room where we all just paced the floors; he, too, was crazy with worry. Doing nothing was torture; we couldn't even notify the police because she had not been missing long enough. This infuriated me, as if I didn't know something hadn't happened to her! It seemed so stupid. We went through a hopeful hell waiting for the proper amount of time to pass and praying she would somehow be home with us before that.

Since doing nothing was unbearable, Dan and I started our own search. It took hours, but we finally found the street address of the girl Terry went shopping with. I was positive we would find them both sound asleep and had already planned what I would say to her. I was curious to know what had happened that would ever keep her from calling us. No one answered the door, so we walked around the house, peeking in all the windows looking for two sleeping forms or clothing that belonged to Terry on any of the beds. It seemed no one was home, but Terry's friend pulled in the driveway as we headed for our car. We almost screamed in unison, "God, where in the world is Terry?" Her reply froze the blood in my veins. "Gee, I don't know where Terry is. I had an accident yesterday and had to go to the emergency room, so I wasn't here when Terry came to pick me up. She left me a note saying, "Shame on you for not being home, see you tomorrow at work," Love, Terry."

Oh, dear God, what could have happened? Where was she?

I called my husband from a phone booth and told him what we had just found out, but he kept saying not to worry. He was sure she was all right. You, who read this, who have gone through this nightmare, the blur of events that followed was precisely that. God in His mercy puts your whole body on "numb."

Dan and I retraced her steps to the mall after leaving her friend's house, and there, in front of JC Penney's, where she and I would always park, sat her car alone in the vast empty parking lot that would soon be filling up with the first of the early morning shoppers. It looked lost without her.

Realizing we might destroy fingerprints on the car, Dan and I only opened the door and looked in for a sign of anything. Terry had a folded change of clothes on the back seat, something she always carried because of her shift work schedule. Nothing else was different. By this time, the mall opened, and we went in, going to all the stores we knew she frequented and asked clerks to identify her from photographs we both carried in our wallets. Dan took one side of the mall and I the other. Finally, we found one clerk who had waited on Terry and could even tell us what she bought. That was as close as we came to finding out anything. The police and the F.B.I. would later do the rest. There is little recollection now of what filled the hours and the days to follow.

Early the following day, I went to a local printing shop with a recent picture of Terry. I had a thousand posters made, which we distributed with the help of our friends throughout Brevard County to every gas station, store, bank, movie, or bar that might post it, and they all did. It seemed everyone in the world was looking for Terry.

That evening Don and I went to the mall to meet the local authorities at Terry's car. The police fingerprinted everything and summoned a locksmith to make a set of keys so it could be moved. It was cold that night, and I stood there shivering, not feeling anything but sensing that this was not really happening. It couldn't be; this was a dream. How many times in the months to follow was I to believe again and again that this was just a bad dream and at any moment I would wake up and tell Terry about it, and we'd laugh about the whole thing … but I never woke up.

Standing there that night watching the curious shoppers turn their heads on the way to their cars, how I envied them their detachment. I felt I would never know this detachment again, ever. Fearing the most precious thing in my whole life may have been taken away, left me with a void that has no description. The emptiness and physical pain hurt so much you want to take a pain pill but don't. You do, however, become acutely aware of other people's pain and suffering after your loss has subsided. It is akin to belonging to an elite club that only those who have suffered the same hell are eligible for membership; others can only imagine its initiation.

I drove Terry's car home that night after the police were through with it. Her car was so much a part of her it gave me comfort to be in it. My insides smiled as I looked at the gas gauge, on empty as usual. When we would go somewhere together in her car, it drove me crazy to look at that gas gauge. Terry would always slough it off, saying, "Oh Mom, we have plenty of gas!"

And somehow, she never ran out. Driving home now, in the deepest part of me, the part that stays hidden, I knew I would never see her again, but I would not allow myself those definite thoughts. Why add more pain to the pain already welling up inside of me? Sometimes we all "know" things before we "know" them. I know I "knew," but I wasn't ready to face it.

There were a lot of people around by that time. Friends had found out and were stopping by just for the sake of saying they cared. During those awful nights, Dan slept in the living room, curled up on the couch, clutching Terry's teddy bear as if that stuffed toy would miraculously bring her back. The sight of this handsome, pathetic-looking young man lying there so desolately tore me up. But, strangely enough, it was Terry's boyfriend, Dan, who was the greater part of my strength during all of this. My husband Don, was methodically doing his own searching with the help of all our personal friends and those in law enforcement.

The other person who was always there was my best friend Lorraine, who, after my first call that Terry was missing, drove over from Tampa and never left my side through the entire nightmare. She was the only one I felt who knew what I was going through, every feeling and every thought, every pain, for she had four daughters.

The period between when Terry was missing and when she was found seemed endless to me, but that night before it became official, the telephone rang around three in the morning. Don answered, said something, and hung up, I asked him what the call was about, and he said, just some problem at the department. It was a report from the Polk County Sheriff's office saying they had found the body of a young woman fitting Terry's description a few days before, and it now lay unidentified in their morgue. The description fit our daughter to a "T." So he wouldn't alarm me any more than was necessary, Don feigned sleep and left for work as usual, hoping that it wasn't Terry. Long before it was time for him to come home for lunch, his car rolled into the driveway. Hearing his car, I went out to meet him, always hoping, always inquiring. He looked pale, and suddenly I noticed how much older he looked. I never remembered his hair so gray. He just stood there by his car with a small piece of paper in his hand. It was a computer printout describing the body they had found. It was our Terry.

Was it a hundred years before this moment I sat in the Sheriff's office giving them my description of her? Do you know how it feels, describing the body of your child and identifying scars? How I knew each one: a scar on her right foot when she banged into a broken full-length mirror a few years ago and the rush to the hospital for stitches, another scar on her leg when she mistakenly stood too near a motorcycle when it was starting up, and the almost imperceptible scars on her face from the chickenpox when she was six. Then there were two small toes that curled beneath the other, one on each foot, exactly like mine. We used to kid about the fact that that was our only resemblance.

My world stopped there in the driveway with my

husband and that piece of paper. We held each other and cried. Whoever was in the house at the time came out. I don't remember anyone other than Mom and Dan, but I think my older sister was there by then too. Thank God I've forgotten certain times in that period. Questions erupted. How did she die? Could we see her? Who could have killed her and why?

There were four of us who picked out Terry's coffin and the cemetery in which she would be buried: Lorraine, Dan, my older sister, and myself. The coffin had to be closed. Terry had been badly beaten on the day she disappeared, then thrown in a creek where a lineman who had climbed a pole to do some repairs had found her three days later.

If it weren't for this man, our hell would have been even worse. We at least had the privilege of burying our daughter. Others have not been so fortunate, and my heart went out to them.

There were questions and more questions. No, I couldn't see her, it would not be possible. But now I sometimes wish I could have just touched her hand or stroked her hair, just one touch to say goodbye. Maybe it was best after all. We all came into the house as my brother-in-law, Bob, pulled into the driveway after driving straight through from Massachusetts. All he knew was that Terry was missing. When I told him, Bob was out of the car and just put his head down on the car's roof and cried. Bob had always kidded Terry about her sweet tooth because she was a "chocoholic" from the word "go" and would devour Hostess Devil Dogs when she was up on Cape Cod visiting. When they knew Terry would be coming up, they would stock their freezer with this particular treat. (The last thing to be placed on Terry's casket at the cemetery was put there by Bob. It was her beloved Devil Dog.)

That night the rest of the family arrived, numb and heartbroken. Disbelief and tears filled the night.

In this time frame, a suspect was found, one who was wanted in connection with two other missing young women from the Miami area. His name meant nothing to me. It was just a name, Christopher Wilder. Local and national news had the story on at every newsbreak of the day from the time she was declared missing through the entire case. The search for Christopher Wilder became the most intensive manhunt in history, but they didn't catch him soon enough—Not in time for the other families just like ours.

It would not be until August that completed tests on blood and hair samples found in Wilder's abandoned car would prove conclusively that Terry's body had been in the trunk of his Chrysler convertible.

CHAPTER THREE

A STRANGER IN MY BODY HELPED the priest with wake and funeral arrangements. Though thousands of flowers absorbed what they could of the tears, jostling for their own space, spilling out of the room into the hall with breathtaking colors, opulence, and love; there was no holding back the grief. Terry's casket was covered solidly with hundreds of pink rosebuds, her final blanket. Flowers marked each pew down the aisle. There was not room for one more flower. Two recent photographs of Terry smiled out over the roses. Dan's huge broken-heart floral arrangement rested with all his dreams to the right-hand side of the casket at her feet.

If Terry had been a princess out of Grimm's Fairy Tales, her wake and funeral could not have been more beautiful or impressive. Making these arrangements for Terry was uppermost in my mind and heart to make it as light as possible. Her death was sad enough, and I knew she would not want a somber, tear-jerking mass or wake service. I wanted the message to be full of hope and promise, not bogged down in despair because all her young friends were there. I wanted them to have something to identify with, something they could relate to, if possible. Recent popular songs were played at her mass the following morning, and in retrospect had I thought of it, I would have had them play one of Michael Jackson's songs. Terry adored him and his music and had planned to go to his concert when he toured Orlando that coming summer.

In discussing the funeral arrangements with the priest, we discussed Terry's religious beliefs. I told him, in all honesty, I did not know what she actually believed. I knew she did not believe as I did. From conversations over the years, I knew she did not have my unwavering faith in God. She questioned everything that I always took for granted. He assured me that if she had led a good life, she was kind and thoughtful to her parents and friends, this was what mattered. She lived what she was, but it could never be called religious. Terry never talked about God to me, and frankly, I don't think she bought the whole package but didn't want to hurt my feelings by telling me so. Although Terry went to church with me until recent years and was raised Catholic, she was not the same Catholic as I remember being.

First Holy Communion

Maybe it was a sign of the times, but a Catholic was a breed apart in the fifties. In the seventies and eighties, it was not so. My thoughts drifted back to Terry's First Holy Communion. I shall never forget the awkward dilemma I found myself in with her. She refused to confess her sins to the priest as was required. As shy and introverted as she was at that age, Terry was adamant that she would tell God directly if she had done something wrong. Finally, a visit with our understanding pastor granted her the right to receive Holy Communion sans confession. She was about seven years old. I would never have dared think about such a thing at her age, much less had the courage to speak and refuse! When Terry was about twelve years old, she told me once that she wanted to have the faith that I did, but no matter how hard she prayed, nothing happened. All I could say to her was that faith would come. My beliefs were simple: believe everything taught without question. If the church said something was so, that was it. Who was I to question learned men?

Before the wake, people would kneel in front of her casket as was customary, saying a brief prayer. It was seeing her young friends that broke my heart. Here were the faces I had seen so many times flying in and out of our house, both male and female, now seeing the two pictures placed on her coffin and sobbing their insides out. When they came to see me, it was I that consoled them, holding them and hugging each of them in turn. Some of her friends would get within a few feet of her casket, break down, and go weeping back to where they had been sitting. They were trying so hard to be grown up. After a brief service, a retired priest and family friend read Terry's eulogy.

The words he spoke were down-to-earth and heartfelt by all. However, those that stayed alive in my memory were these profound words; "Something is afoot in the universe, something resembling gestation and birth. The resurrection of Jesus gives us assurance, par excellence, that something truly is afoot in the universe, that the life of man, every man, has eternal significance."

At her funeral the following day, March 27, the priest kept his message light and full of hope, but I could not actually grasp the fact that Terry was in the coffin as it sat there waiting for mass, and nor could I when we followed it up the aisle after mass ended. The funeral procession, covered in part by television stations and newspaper reporters, was one of the most impressive displays Brevard

County had ever seen. It was led by uniformed police officers on motorcycles riding abreast, representing various departments throughout the area.

We rode out of the church parking lot to the main road, across the river connecting the beach area to the mainland where her burial would take place. Upon reaching the other side of the bridge and the main road, a police officer stood at attention, saluting as the hearse passed by. At every intersection was an officer halting traffic and standing at attention. That's when I heard you for the first time! I heard you say, "Mom, I'm impressed!" Law enforcement cleared all traffic for the last fifteen miles to let us through. Terry's final ride was that of a queen, sparing nothing. She never thought of herself as well-liked or even slightly popular. Here was a tribute she could never have imagined.

Now, looking back, I multiply our sorrow by the thousands across the nations of the world, the senseless murders, and the innocent, unknowing victims. The screams of torment venting when the pain from a heart becomes so great only a cry from the soul releases the pressure. How many screams are there? And they are all the same, 'Why him? Why her? Why them?' Many questions seem worse when the victim and murderer do not even know each other. The big unanswered question is always "why?" After a loss so great, there is no returning to who you were; you will never be the same. This is not to say you will not be a much better person, a stronger person, or a more understanding person, for you will be. It is up to you from this point onward. It helps to realize that placing the blame and hating wastes precious emotions and energy that turn inward and punish your body, not those they are directed to. The actual answer to "why" came later as a jolt, an unexpected one, and with it, brought complete understanding. There it was... Truth... shimmering in the light. It wasn't visible to me until years later when my mind could digest, accept and totally understand it.

With the candle vigil outside of death row before an execution gives rise to another question. If people object to the death penalty, and consider the condemned, a victim himself, why don't they burn another candle for those whose lives was taken? If Christopher Wilder were to have survived or ever made it to the point of execution, I would go among those candles and let my tears extinguish the flames. This would be my final balance. Though tears flow from the eyes, their source is most certainly the heart. Most of those on death row have been there for many years, exercising their rights, getting trials, retrials, and stays of execution. What an imbalance of justice that the victim could not have had the same. I would learn later that there was indeed a balance after all.

To the legal system, Terry was just one of the millions of young women in the country and one more daughter who never made it home alive. Her murderer was under psychiatric care and out on probation from a 1980 rape case in which the judge withheld adjudication. I wonder how that judge feels now. Wilder was arrested in Australia in the December 1982 rape of a teenager in New South Wales and charged later for misrepresenting himself as a photographer for a Palm Beach talent agency. The case was set for April 1984. He was released on a $350,000.00 bond. Because of his arrest in the Australian rape case, he was charged with violating his Palm Beach probation. Wilder's attorney said he was reasonably confident that the violation was about to be dismissed. Wilder was very corporative and had abided by all the conditions of his probation. He; (Wilder) at least realized he had a problem and was under a doctor's care. How many more like him are there roaming the streets who don't even know they have problems?

We can warn our children time and time again. We all have and will continue to do so. But there is nothing you can do to protect your child or someone you love from a madman… nothing except perhaps to seek to radically improve our criminal justice system so that they keep more of these people off the streets.

For the first time in my life, I knew hate. I hated this one man with a frightening intensity. Those feelings gradually wore off as something happened, keeping my mind off Christopher Wilder and focusing on something much more worthwhile. It was a growing awareness of someone I could not see or hear trying to comfort me somehow, a quiet inner peace that rolled over me and took the edge off my pain. If there is but one person reading this now who has experienced that same awareness, who can relate and say, hey, that's how I felt, or that's how I feel, then what I am writing will have served its purpose. That same person will know that they are not alone or crazy, for the topic I am about to address is one we don't openly discuss.

I'm talking about communication with those that are deceased. It happens more than most people know, and many of us have had many experiences that we just don't talk about for fear of being looked at questionably. There are so many ways that loved ones reach out to us, hoping we will know they still exist, still love us, and still live on. We have been taught to expect nothing as far as communication is concerned. We certainly have not been taught, nor has it been suggested that when someone dies, communication is possible. At least I hadn't, so you too may find your own religion challenging your heart's belief system. Follow your intuition.

The bible does not say we cannot communicate with the dead; it says we should not. But what would you do if someone you loved just died and you sensed they were trying to tell you something? Would you ask them to just "go away?" I don't think so. I had never given much thought to this myself. After all, who goes around thinking things like that? Most minds are full of everyday problems and things to be done from morning to night, and unless confronted with it, they would not give such a thing any thought. Crazy titles on tabloids at the supermarket checkout stands would headline these incidents, but it never made me buy one. There was no believing nor disbelieving with me. I just didn't care one way or another. If I got down to the bottom line, did I think it could happen? Sure, why not? But there was nothing like that taught at church on Sunday, that's for sure. Never in all my life had I ever heard it mentioned in church, and I'm wondering why?

It reminded me of one of my painting instructors and one lesson stuck in my mind. It was an impressionistic painting class, different from the others in that we did not paint what we had come to expect as reality. Instead, our teacher trained us to look for what was not obvious and strive to see colors, where at first glance, there were none. She taught us to stay away, color-wise, from our first visual impact and look beyond until we saw something else. When we became trained to see beyond what we 'saw,' the whole world glowed and throbbed with new excitement, color, and wonder... and so it is with this thing we call death and communication with those that have left this earth. It exists as surely as God does, but we sadly lack the training to embrace it.

My teaching advocated praying for the deceased, and praying to God to help us through our sorrow, but why has no one taught us to listen? By listening, I mean a more profound listening than that to which we have accustomed ourselves. I'm not talking about sounds and voices as we hear them. What I am referring to is the tuning into our own voice within us. How many times have you heard someone say, relating to someone who has died, that in certain instances shortly afterward that they could almost hear that person saying this or that in their mind? Or something pops into your head all of a sudden, you imagined a picture of that person, and he or she seems so alive. It gave you the feeling that they were really there for that second in time, were actually thinking of you, and communicating this in a way that they could from their consciousness to your mind. Since Terry died, I have been examining the possibilities of "what if" and finding my search fascinating, frustrating, and even funny.

* * *

Trying to remember the first time I felt Terry's presence is challenging, but definitely, she was with both Don and me at her wake. Feelings or sensations were overcoming us at certain moments that defy description. It was as if something slipped inside of me and filled me up to the top with warmth. There was a feeling of peace, the hurt disappeared, and I knew something was happening, but at the same time, I couldn't label it. Now I can. It was Terry or God or both, for how could one be without the other?

How many people have experienced this sensation? How many have had strange little things happen in their home after death and dare not talk of them because of what people would think or say, so they write it off as an overactive imagination? This something we are afraid to talk about or mention and that we are so ashamed to even believe in is God, but certainly, this is a part of God that has never been taught or discussed at church, and again I wonder why? As a Christian, I had always believed that Christ appeared to his friends after his death. But does it state that He was the only one who would do this? If life everlasting was the gift He gave, then wouldn't it seem likely that others who have died could make themselves known to their loved ones somehow, though not exactly in the physical sense? Why not? What if the mind and soul were tied together with God, and imagination was a part of it? Even as I write it, I cannot clearly explain how this works, but I know they are somehow tied together. If we believe there is someplace after death, do we ever imagine where? Where does everyone go? As Terry's mother, I always knew where she was while she was on this earth, or at least I tried to. This desire to know did not end with her death. I do not believe that death could be the end of that spirit that she was, the love she lavished on her friends, and the great sense of humor she shared with us. As a flame dancing in the wind turns into smoke, I wondered what form Terry took and where she was if she still existed in the state after death.

At the most tragic moment of my life, something held me together; there was an inner strength that suddenly manifested itself. The sorrow was there, but equal to it was this inner strength. For the longest time, I just assumed I was still in shock. Many have felt that shock, the pain, and the torment after losing what feels like half of ourselves. How many others have felt what I became more and more attuned to: that someone was trying to get through to me. It was as if someone was knocking on my door, but I hadn't been listening.

There is no convincing some of the possibilities of life after death. If the mind is closed to this idea, it does not seek more information on the subject. Why should it? I had entertained the idea myself before but had never probed into it. My mind was always open to different things like flying saucers and life on other planets, but I never investigated such beliefs. They simply existed and were as fundamental as my belief in God. Why think any more about it? But for all my faith in God, the ensuing months were the most confusing in my life, and pain was a nagging companion.

As April approached, our lives were in a major upheaval, seeking Terry's murderer. It obsessed Don and me both. I hated this man and eagerly watched and waited for news of him as he crossed the country abducting and murdering other young women.

April 13, 1984. At a small gas station in Colebrook, New Hampshire, a state trooper cautiously approached a vehicle. The man in the driver's seat matched Wilder's description. When asked for identification, the man reached over to the glove compartment withdrawing instead, a 357 magnum handgun. Quickly the officer grabbed Wilder's arm, the struggle was brief. Two shots fired. One shot wounded the police officer, the other turned inward, killing Wilder immediately.

It was over.

The news bulletin broke on every major television network, "Christopher Wilder, shot to death trying to escape into Canada."

I had no idea Terry's death would impact anyone else's personal life at this point, other than that of our immediate family. However, this certainly was not so, for a woman I had never met was already experiencing ripples, set in motion by the tidal wave of Terry's death.

Friends recommended a well-known parapsychologist and psychic named Rose during Terry's disappearance to assist us in locating her. Don had talked with her many times, and I was only vaguely aware of these calls. There were so many calls from so many people; no one could keep track of them. Rose had told Don that Terry's body would be found in a swampy area, and she was at peace. She told him Terry did not suffer greatly and that she had been in touch with her. Hearing the words, "she did not suffer greatly," brought relief, but how was I to be sure? Do we just believe what we want to believe? What if it was not true? Does it become truth after we believe it? Do we create our own reality?

I had to know. To do this, I needed to personally meet the source of this information to determine how much credence there was to these peaceful and comforting messages. Quickly we arranged a meeting, and on April 4th, a few weeks after Terry's death, with mixed feelings, Don and I drove to the city of Orlando for this consultation. To me, personally, it was of the utmost importance what I saw when I met this woman, for I was cautious about the whole thing. Nonetheless, whoever she was, she had given me a large degree of tranquility that had carried me over some excruciating days with the information she had told us about Terry following her death.

Rose was not what I had anticipated, but I don't really know what I was expecting. She was younger than I with a bubbly personality, a friendly smile, and a definite twinkle in her blue eyes. I liked her immediately and felt I had known her for a long time. Don said he felt the same way. Rose told us that Terry was there in the room with us and had communicated with her many times. She wanted us to know she was okay. We were told that Terry was still very homesick; she missed her life and us but that she was adjusting. As Rose talked and I listened, I also was playing the role of a doubting Thomas.

How could I know for sure that this was all true? I was questioning everything at this point, though I said nothing. Then Rose looked at me and said, "You want proof Terry is here, don't you?" I nodded my head because I did need proof. Rose told us that Terry had just said that she did not like the picture of her we put in the paper. (It had truly been the worst picture of her we had ever seen, but in the confusion of her disappearance, this was the picture given to the press.) Terry told us not to grieve too much. She thanked us for a good life and for all we had done. She said that she had been with us constantly since she had died.

We both asked Rose many questions about many things, all pertaining in one way or another to Terry and how this communication could be. Even though our questions were answered, some answers I didn't understand. One thing we were told I understood perfectly; we were to talk to Terry just as we would if she were here in the physical because she was with us and could hear whatever we had to say. She could hear our mental conversations as well. I wanted to know why I could not hear any answer, for what were one-sided questions and conversations? Rose told me to speak with my mind and to imagine what her reply would be. That was fine, but how could I distinguish between what she would say from what I would pretend I was hearing? That, to me, was like carrying on a conversation with myself and pretending it was Terry. How was I to know? Rose told me I would definitely know because an answer would come into my head, and I would be positive that I did not put it there. She was right. When it happened the first time, I smiled like the Cheshire cat, smug and all-knowing. This experience gave me the sensation that my heart just smiled, then broke into a grin.

Our conversation with Rose lasted about an hour and left Don and me feeling lighthearted and actually happy for the first time since Terry died. We wanted to celebrate in a special way, so we went to a jewelry store to pick out something I had always wanted: a pair of diamond studs for my ears. Some of Terry's own savings were to pay for part of them, the rest from Don. So now I had something from both of them, and they will always be more than special to me. When I tried to decide which pair to buy, the thought crossed my mind to think about it and come back another day. It was then I heard Terry's quite aggravated voice in my head, "Mum, for heaven's sake, buy the damn earrings now, or you never will!" So, I bought the earrings and we left.

After buying the earrings, we stopped at a nearby restaurant for lunch. We had finished devouring food for our minds and souls, and now we needed to nourish our bodies. We entered the restaurant and were met by the waitress, who asked, "How many?" I replied, "Three please," while beaming at Don. The waitress gave a look behind me, looking for the third, shrugged, and led us to a table for three where we had a fabulous meal.

CHAPTER FOUR

FROM THE FIRST DAY WE met Rose, things were never quite the same, but I cannot pinpoint the exact day I knew something very different was going on with me. The first related incident that I was aware of began sometime in May. While having morning coffee with Don, I noticed my coffee cup seemed to move while my hand was on it. Thinking moisture was responsible for the sliding cup, I kept moving it back to where it was, wiping it off and feeling it slide away again. I don't know how long this took place before I showed Don my "moving cup." He showed little interest and went back to reading the paper. I was mesmerized and wondered if small objects could move too. When I put my hands lightly on bottle caps, paper clips, or pens lying down on their sides, they would glide around in swirls and loops. But now what? And, so what?

One morning Don was suddenly, and for no apparent

reason, impressed with an idea. He suggested I get a piece of paper, put a pen in my hand, and see what might happen. I did so, and within seconds I unconsciously began to move my hand at random, wafting over the paper in easy, sweeping, gently curving lines. It was fun and captivating, but where was it coming from? Was it me? Well, it was me, but, consciously, for the life of me, I could not figure out why this was going on. Before long, there were pages and pages of drawings all over the house. One of the simplest designs was that of a figure eight on its side. Some of the others looked like a form of vegetation from another planet.

Showing my drawings to friends brought on disbelieving looks and sympathetic nods, implicating "I had lost my only child and my mind to boot." What else could cause a reasonably ordinary woman to start doing things like this? I discovered talking to others could be a big mistake. Now I understand why no one wants to talk about a lot of other things. After that first time, my hand always did something when I had a pen in it, so I made sure that I was prepared with enough paper to last me whenever I was home sitting down alone. Then one day, again at the breakfast table while having morning coffee, I felt like picking up the pen. This time I was stunned when my pen started to write sentences!

When I wasn't writing sentences, I would write, "Love, Terry," and when I was writing it the first time, I burst out crying because it was in her handwriting! I knew it was her. I felt it! Even immersed in the morning paper, I felt Don's curiosity begin to peak as I caught him from time to time, lower his paper and glance my way as my hand swept objects slowly around the table. He knew I wouldn't write the things that I was writing. Instead, I would write the word "question," which would be followed by a question. One such query was, "Who frees the man who knows no bonds?" I figure whoever was doing the writing was waiting for an answer, so I consciously wrote, "No one." I guess I got that one wrong because my hand unconsciously wrote, "Himself."

My mind was in a constant quandary, and this was the most puzzling thing that had ever happened to me. What did all this mean? Was I losing my mind? The shock of Terry's death may well have done damage I was not able to comprehend. Was this the result? I had to know what was going on, and trying to find the answers was not easy. Who could I turn to? Most people I talked to told me it was only my imagination, that I was really subconsciously doing it.

There was only one person I felt a definite feeling of trust with, and that was Rose. I made an appointment to see her again and, placing all my saved-up papers with squiggles and loops in front of her, awaited a verdict with great trepidation. But instead, she smiled as she rifled through my drawings and pronounced me sane. She herself had experienced the same thing early in her development, particularly the figure eight design lying on its side. She told me this meant my mind was open, and someone was successful in getting through to me. By this time, I had no doubt who it was, for whenever I plunged into sadness over Terry's death and had a pen in my hand, it wrote, "Love, Terry."

What dumbfounded me though, was that it was in her handwriting and not mine. Our handwriting is distinctly different. Every time my hand wrote her little message, I smiled away my tears. For reasons beyond my comprehension, Terry still "was." Somehow, somewhere, she existed, and although I could not see her with my eyes, I felt her presence assuredly as if she were there. After the greatest sorrow of my life, my heart already knew, that I had to be objective and keep an open mind to all sides. To accept something without researching the other possibilities was foolhardy to me, and it still is. Life after death was never taught in my religious upbringing, and it had never been spoken of in this way. How much easier we could handle death if we all realized that we do not go "up" or "down" after dying." We continue to exist in another life within this realm; it is as real as this one. Many people are content with just knowing something happens after we die, but my search goes further and will continue.

Rose explained to me that automatic writing is accomplished in one of three ways: one, by using the intuition to pull forth information from one's higher levels of consciousness, two, intuitively receiving messages from other individuals or entities and transcribing them, or three, by allowing a disembodied entity to use your body to relay messages through the written word. The first two are relatively safe and fascinating as you discover limitless power. The last method is not only limiting but also dangerous. Anytime you leave yourself open to lower psychic forces or even to the suggestion of stronger minds, you risk losing a part of your own identity and control of your mental faculties. She told me I did a little of each, at times tapping into my own higher sources of knowledge, sometimes intuitively communicating with Terry and at other times allowing Terry to use my body to sign, "Love, Terry."

CHAPTER FIVE

A FEW SHORT WEEKS AFTER TERRY'S death, her boyfriend Dan resumed classes at the Florida Institute of Technology, where he majored in computer marketing. It was a painful struggle trying to continue his studies and life without Terry. I hurt so for him. I knew how much they had loved one another, and now he was suddenly alone. His family lived in Connecticut, and although his mother and best friend Steve came down for Terry's funeral, they could only stay for so long.

Nevertheless, Dan remained close through the months to follow, coming for dinner often, drawn like a magnet to our home where he and Terry had shared so much. Once in the house, inevitably, Dan would wander into her room and just sit. There were times when I went in and sat beside him on Terry's bed and put my arm around his shoulder, saying nothing. There were times when I left him alone.

There were days we could not believe it, and there still are. Dan shared a side of Terry that I was not fully aware of and gave me some insight into some of the things that made her so lovable and what she would do to please those she loved. A month before Terry was killed, on February 13th, Valentine's Day eve, late after work, she strung a thirty-foot handmade banner across the balcony of his dorm saying simply, "I love you, Terry". She had done this for his birthday too. Terry delighted in surprising friends with birthday presents, wrapped and earmarked appropriately for each one. I would always marvel at the amount of thought, time, and money she would put into these little love offerings.

Terry's friends were the populace of her world, and she was its nucleus, radiating energy and love to those around her. I missed the comings and goings of her friends, especially weekends when they would all go out dancing at the local Holiday Inn. Her friends would come over to borrow or swap clothes during these times, and she would put on their makeup with great expertise. Terry loved making up her friends and took great pride in the outcome. She had hoped to make cosmetology a career and majored in business in college. She would tell me many things she and her friends would do, the fun they would have, and both she and I would laugh together over these shared experiences.

She and I were as close as two people could be. We shared our lives without prying, and we were aware of each other's loves and interests. When time allowed, we shared. When it did not, we understood. After her workday, when she would come home, I always dropped whatever I was doing, and we would just have a session and talk over whatever our mutual day entailed. We'd throw thoughts around, back and forth to each other, responding only when each would feel the necessity. Terry was one of the best listeners I have ever met in my life. She listened, really listened. There are very few people who actually do this. Most just simply pretend, while all the time, formulating in their minds what they want to say. I could tell her about anything; she was one of my best friends. When there was a need to talk, we both were always there for one another. It was an essential part of our relationship and one I treasured.

It would be almost a year before I realized how much Terry's death had affected her friends. As the newspaper said shortly after her death, "a very special woman was plucked from their lives." As a mother, what I felt was one thing, but I could put my grief aside and see how devastated her friends were. They were all Terry's age, around twenty-one, and had never experienced a loss, much less of a friend their own age. Their world had been shaken to the core, their faith, if they had any, put to the test. I wondered how they were faring.

Terry had many male friends from the seventh grade on through graduation, some she dated, some just friends, but friends they were, and it was these young men who stopped by the house after the turmoil quieted down. During semester breaks from colleges out of town or on leave from the military, they stopped by just to say "Hi" and talk over old times, those with funny memories. They will never know, unless they read this book, how much their little visits touched me, how good it made me feel to know they still thought of her and would bother to take the time to stop by.

Her girlfriends shied away at first. They wore their hearts on their sleeves and were afraid of their emotions. Finally, after many months, one friend came by and what she said made me realize how much they hurt too. I had been so wrapped up in my pain I was oblivious to that of others. She told me she could not come before because it hurt so much pulling into the driveway and walking into the house, when every time before, there had been so much happiness with Terry.

I had missed these friends of Terry, for they too were very much a part of my life. I had shared their lives through Terry and them. Terry often told me how much her friends envied her because she and I were so close and had so much fun together. I always came out on top, according to her, when compared to other mothers. Our relationship always made me feel genuinely good. Trying to define such a relationship shared between two people is difficult. It just boils down to love.

I remember asking Rose why I felt torn apart, so cut down the middle, so empty, when Terry was killed. She replied that Terry and I had previously shared lifetime upon lifetime together and that our lives always touched when major changes or new and good things occurred. For all the happiness Terry had given me in this lifetime, then, I was puzzled.

What great deed was accomplished with her horrible death? She explained that Terry dying in this way gave Don and me an opportunity for tremendous spiritual growth and greater insight into God. Terry had actually raised my level of God-consciousness that I would have struggled to attain on my own. At the time, I felt I would rather have Terry back. Faith, I already had. I did not understand at all what this meant, and it would be years before I did. In this physical reality, I couldn't fathom Terry doing something like this, knowing how much I loved her, but her actions were not born from this physical reality at all. It was her soul, fulfilling its own destiny, as it is with each of us.

Questions formed in my mind. Some of the questions have been answered; others I still seek the answers to. As far as reincarnation was concerned, I had never heard much about it before Rose brought it up in connection to Terry's death. It wasn't that I disbelieve, it was just that I had never given it any thought one way or the other. My upbringing was Catholic. All that mattered to me was my firm belief in God. I personally felt a power existed, a loving and caring one who knew everything and was in complete charge. At this time, I had no idea this power was shared with us, but life is a learning process, and I was on its doorstep.

When I read some books on reincarnation, they fit in with all my beliefs at the time and tied loose ends together. I had always wondered how a good and loving God could allow such horrors in the world. Reincarnation supplied the answers, and God still came out on top. With reincarnation, the belief is that you come here to learn specific lessons chosen by yourself before you are born. Once learning and experiencing what you came to experience, you go "home." You may be one month old or one hundred years old, time itself means nothing.

CHAPTER SIX

THROUGH ALL MY NEW EXPERIENCES, I always talked to Terry, sometimes out loud, sometimes to myself, depending on whether or not I was alone. It was as if we consoled each other. Once or twice a day, I would sit down with pen and paper and ask her if she had a message for me. Her answer, drawn with a flourish by me, would most always be a big heart. There was no problem understanding that! I drew a heart once, with my initials on top. Then, I wrote the word "loves" in the middle and her initials underneath and asked if she could top that. My hand immediately drew a heart and reversed the initials. We laughed together. All pain flew out the window during these little sessions.

There were times too that I knew it was not Terry with whom I was communicating. I sensed the difference. One was a sensation of love and fun, which was Terry. There was a sensation of love with the other, but added to it was knowledge, or I think a better word would be "wisdom." I would learn later that this was my higher consciousness. Writing and asking questions each day brought little reprimands, a subtleness, but I got the message. In the midst of one of my morning writings came the question to me, "Why don't you just listen?" Easier said than done, but I started working on it. Soon feelings of Terry's presence began to become the ordinary instead of the unexpected. Her absence was known to me, physically and mentally, but in my heart her presence filled that physical void most of the time.

With all these experiences and this great faith of mine, you might think that I would never ever have been sad. From what I knew, I should have always been happy knowing that Terry was not dead but very much alive in another state of existence as we all are when we die. How I wish it worked that way, but it doesn't. I cried a lot. Everyone who has lost someone they love deeply has felt that pain in their chest so severe you wonder what part of your physical body is capable of such suffering. You view the world differently after you've survived a loss. Everything looks different when I look out the window; colors are subdued, and the sky is not as blue. Trees have lost their rich shades of green. It's as though someone had put a haze over everything.

Nothing is in focus anymore, and you wonder where all the beauty has gone. Yet, these same people have felt the pain diminish over a period of months and years, replaced by a dull ache, releasing you finally when you are ready. Gradually the haze lifts, and not being able to pinpoint a day, the realization comes that the world never changed at all. It is still beautiful, and clarity returns. It was us, not the world, that was out of focus. And no matter what our faith or belief may be, we still are held from time to time in the grips of grief. It strikes without warning when our defenses are down, endless reminders of things that were and will not be again; a certain walk, the color of someone's hair, a fleeting expression on someone else, will open memory's door. These memories can be wonderful, but it's best if they are controlled, lest they control you… for the power they hold is unbelievable.

One memory of thousands I have of Terry took place a few years ago. My mind plays re-runs of it often when a particular song plays on the radio. As a needle is to the record, so this song is to my heart. It was our city employees' Christmas party at a local restaurant. Don and I were there and asked Terry to stop by on her way home with her date and join us for a drink. She and her date did drop by for a few minutes, talked with us, and were about to leave when the band played this song. They headed for the dance floor, Terry's home away from home. They were both fantastic! I had never seen Terry dance before, and I was fascinated and proud at the same time. My eyes riveted on her as she whirled into step, never missing a beat while joy and concentration mixed with life's blush shone on her face. Magic surrounded her as she moved in exultation on the dance floor; dark hair flying with momentum, precision movements flashing their intensity, softened between the music's beat with instinctive pauses, then quickening again until the tangle of notes ended. Terry had embraced life, quenching her thirst for the moment. Now she dances only on the dance floor of my mind, but it is still a beautiful scene. Whenever I hear that song now, I fall apart. Sometimes I felt ashamed when I cried, knowing she was around. For a brief time, twenty-one years, Terry had given me herself, the most beautiful gift of all, and now I would be experiencing her and loving her in a whole new way.

It was June, a few months after Terry was killed. I had seen Rose twice and talked to her on the telephone many times. Perplexing things were going on all around me, and with every new event, I called and asked her to explain what was going on. How fortunate for me that we had met. I would not have known whom to turn to if it had not been for her always being there and only a phone call away. In addition, she had sent me two pocketbooks to read to answer some of my questions. Both books dealt with past lives and relationships and how they may affect our present lives. Dick Sutphen, a well-known lecturer and famous psychic researcher at the time, wrote the books. They helped me begin to understand so much more. Since I asked Rose so many questions, all directly or indirectly to do with Terry, I felt the need for Rose to know her and know something about her.

The only way I could think of was to mail her some special things Terry had written. I needed Rose to know that Terry was not just a pretty face, and I don't know why else I did it. At the time, it just seemed natural. When Rose read what I had mailed her, she returned them to me with the note: "Dear Fran, thanks for sharing Terry with me. What a kid! She is a writer after my own heart, and I love her for it. I have a very close bond with Terry for reasons I'll probably never put into words, and I am grateful to her for what she has done. With much love and appreciation, Rose." The last sentence gave me a slight case of chills. I didn't understand then the meaning of the note, and by the time I had received it, other things that I questioned even more, had started.

CHAPTER SEVEN

INTERMITTENTLY, THERE WERE TIMES WHEN Terry's unseen presence brought lightness to the atmosphere throughout the house; sadness banishes as if she herself could stand it no longer. By now, Don and I were both known to smile when a light would snap on after we had just turned it off. We could almost hear that silly giggle of hers and see the sparkle of merriment in her eyes. Walking into the guest room one afternoon, announcing her presence with the energy Terry now was, the overhead fan set in the off position gave a couple of full speed circles, and happiness flooded the room.

There were many such interchanges of joy, always catching me unaware but very few people to share them with. It was such a brand-new experience for us, the writing, the small incidences that went on, and Terry was just warming up. She had our attention. We were aware of her being around and any doubts that might arise, dispelled quickly.

Days tiptoed through the calendar, proceeding to every new untouched dawn. Life itself was in a constant state of renewal. Dan would drop by at least once a week, either after classes or on his way to the beach. He'd grab a diet soda, and we'd sit at the kitchen table where the conversation drifted as usual to Terry, but these were always comforting talks. Before he left, he would ramble into Terry's room and wander back out. Everything was exactly as she had left it and would be for months to come, even the pictures she had of him hanging on the wall at the foot of her bed.

It seemed although I knew Terry had been murdered, that it just could not have happened. It just couldn't have! Even though Terry made me aware she was still in existence somewhere, it still seemed impossible to me that she would never again come bouncing through the front door and charge into her room!

Dan was in his last week of finals and studying hard. He would be going home soon for summer vacation as soon as the testing was over. His best friend, Steve, was to fly down from Connecticut to drive home with him. June 5th, the night before Steve flew in, Dan came to our house for dinner as he had many times over the past few months. The atmosphere was always cheerful and light whenever he visited, probably because Terry was there. Terry was usually brought up, but we kept away from the bad memories and talked over all the good ones, all in pleasant connotations.

When it was time for Dan to head back to his dormitory, I got up and walked out with him, a habit I had acquired during Terry's disappearance. I would walk him to his car and wave him off. Until we strolled to his car, this evening was no different from all the rest. Stars studded the clear night sky and it was a particularly lovely evening. There was even a sense of peace in the soft breeze. I remember thinking of the lyric in a song I used to hear at folk masses, "Whenever two or more of you are gathered in my name, there is love." It was a song written by Noel Stookey, called The Wedding Song. Why that flashed through my mind, I don't know. The next moment I was saying good night to Dan. As usual, I kissed him on the cheek, said "Good night, dear," but as our eyes met, I continued with, "I love you, Dan."

He said, "I know. I love you too."

As I turned to walk back up the driveway, I froze. Time stood still. Dan, too, froze where he stood. The hair on our arms stood up as though being hit with an electrical charge. I had never told Dan that I loved him. It was Terry's voice, not mine. She had found a way to deliver her message to her beloved Dan through me. We had been caught so off guard that we were transfixed and remained so for what seemed an eternity, while all I could add was a stupefying "Uh-huh."

Still shaken, Dan turned, got into his car, waved goodbye, and disappeared into the night. The next day I had another message from Terry, and I could hardly wait to share it with him.

As Dan left our house that night, his hand automatically went for the car radio, but as he turned it on, he turned it back off. The radio had become only another painful reminder of what used to be, with music and songs throbbing the hopes, dreams, and feelings once shared by them both. It remained off most of the time now. Driving back this night, his hand reached for the dial, and he corrected himself.

Why ask for more pain or confusion? He fought the feeling on and off, but somehow, he felt compelled to switch it on for reasons he could not understand. Then he knew why. The words, sung by Lionel Richie, filled his heart and the summer darkness, "Hello, is it me you're looking for? Cause I wonder where you are, and I wonder what you do, are you somewhere feeling lonely, or is someone loving you? Tell me how to win your heart, for I haven't got a clue, but let me start by saying, "I love you." The feeling of Terry's presence was so intense he had to pull off the road and, as he said, "I just lost it."

It was the very next morning, on my way to the golf course, when I, too, felt the urgent need to turn on the radio, unaware of Dan's incident the night before. I thought of Terry as I was driving down the highway and wondering about what happened last night. At this point, I did not know that music was but one more way our loved ones give us messages. So, immersing myself in my thoughts, I reached down and turned my radio on. These were the I words I heard, sung by John Lennon; "Woman, I just have to explain, I never meant to cause you sorrow or pain. After all, it was written in the stars, so let me tell you again and again and again, I love you, now and forever."

It would be years later that I would fully understand that "her death was written in the stars." Tears slid down my face, but they were happy tears as I continued on my way to the golf course.

Golf had been my mental savior after Terry died. Without throwing myself entirely into the game and playing four times a week, I would have been in much worse condition. Golf kept me physically busy and mentally exhausted. My pain inside had to be temporarily put aside to engage in this sport. Playing it well required total concentration, and I gave it my all. Only once do I remember leaving the golf course before finishing the round, but one failure out of all my other good days was still a personal triumph. I knew my friends were silently cheering me on, and their support and love made me continue.

Coming home mid-day to the empty house brought me back to reality again, but I kept busy at home too. There was always something to keep me occupied. By this time, I read everything I could get my hands on about life after death experiences: reincarnation, automatic writing, religious articles about the lives of saints, and anything I could find relating to what I had experienced. I took solace because the library shelves were full of such books, so I knew I wasn't alone in my experiences. All these thoughts and ideas were new to me. My need to know filled my every waking moment until sometimes I thought I had lost my mind. There were times when I figured I must have gone off the deep end. Then a voice inside me told me differently and encouraged me to read more, study more, and question more. The depth of my search grew and was so intense, it actually seemed to absorb my pain. Every act of searching for answers felt like it was drawing me closer and closer to Terry. If I found the answers I was looking for, my heart told me I would find my daughter too, wrapped up as a gift within those same answers. In a way, she was.

CHAPTER EIGHT

DAN CALLED ME THE NEXT day to tell me of his emotional ride home, and I told him my story. He reminded me that, as previously planned, he and his friend Steve would be over the following evening to drop off his steamer trunk for storage in Terry's room for the summer.

On the evening of the 7th of June, Dan and Steve lugged the heavy steamer trunk into Terry's room and sat down with my husband and me in the living room. The boys were talking enthusiastically about their upcoming drive to Connecticut. The room's atmosphere was buoyant, almost jovial!

We all talked easily for a few hours, and it was the overall lightness and the closeness we felt that prompted me jokingly to say, "Gee, it's such a perfect evening, everything seems so right. The only one missing is Terry, anyone for a séance?" We all laughed, but Steve said, "Hey, I don't know anything about séances, but I've worked a Ouija Board before."

In retrospect, I know it was no coincidence that I brought this up, and it was no coincidence that Steve was there to follow up on the idea. There are many things I know now that I simply took for granted at the time. Anyway, the only memory I had of the Ouija Board was when I was a child. Every home seemed to have one stuck somewhere in the closet or behind their couch. They were a thing of the past, a child's toy, and we didn't have one, so I suggested making a homemade one.

We tore off a page from a huge desk calendar, turned it over, and had Steve fill in the alphabet letters on the top and put numbers on the bottom. Looking at it, I vaguely remember how the old Ouija Board looked. This was a funny imitation, but we were just having fun anyway. We needed something to rest our fingers on, and I went into Terry's room and took a cover of one of her eye makeup cases. It was transparent, and after my husband smoothed the edges with a bit of sandpaper, it had a good, even surface.

At this point, I remembered we had a houseguest staying in the back bedroom. Heather, Lorraine's daughter, stayed with us for two months. Later I was so grateful for her being there as my mind would need every witness it could muster for what was about to transpire. Heather was doing her homework, but it took no persuasion for her to join us in the living room when I told her what we were doing. By this time, the clock had marched to 10:30 PM Dan's final exams were being held early the following morning, and though he had to be on his way soon, he was willing to try this thing before he left.

Not one of us except Dan's friend had any idea what to expect. Had this been planned with any thought given to positive results, or even any results for that matter, I would have had a tape recorder recording our voices and a camera to show the unbelievable movement propelling our hands.

At first, we put the paper on our coffee table but then realized that it would not give us all a chance to place our hands on the plastic makeup cover. Four of us participated, so we moved it onto the floor and put a section of the glass coffee table over it. My husband sat in his Lazy Boy chair, looking on with mild interest but skeptical amusement, our one doubting Thomas in the room.

Dan's friend began by asking if anyone in the room would like to talk with us. Our hands rested, waiting on the plastic cover for perhaps a minute or two. Nothing happened. Then it began rattling as if dozens of Mexican jumping beans were caught beneath our fingers. Dan's eyebrows shot up. We looked at each other, and we all exchanged glances hurriedly as our hands were drawn to the word "Yes" on the paper. When I say "drawn," it was not a faint or faltering pressure that we experienced. Instead, it was a magnetized force beneath our fingertips so strong we would slide off it if our arms were not in an unencumbered position.

This was not anything like the writing that I would do by myself either; it was much stronger. We all looked at Dan's friend as if to say, "My God, now what?"

Every particle of air was charged as he asked for the first initial of this person's name. There was no hesitation; it was as if the person said, "Hey, at last someone asked!" Our hands went swiftly to the letter T. Tears swam. Could this possibly be? No, it couldn't! Were we doing this collectively? My mind raced, as did the others. Steve then asked for the full name, and our hands went without pausing to "Terry." Our hearts were pounding wildly by now.

We dared not hope. This was impossible, wasn't it? Or was it? We were not kidding ourselves; we all subconsciously knew we were thinking of Terry. Was this all it took to make our hands spell out her name? But our hands were being pulled, not pushed or directed by any of us. It felt like a very powerful magnet beneath the table, and our hands were steel.

We all began asking questions then and admittedly expected profound wisdom from her. Later I learned how foolish this was. Terry was not much more knowledgeable in death than she was while she was on earth with us. The only added knowledge gained at this point was that there is no such thing as death as we know it. Existence goes on. Although this was my first encounter with outwardly communicating with someone who had died, I had by this time read of many such stories and knew it to be possible. In all these stories, those that had died gave different accounts of what their experiences were. There were many deviations, which made me wonder at the time, how they could all think they were right.

The reason for this is simple. Your thoughts are a product of your mind. They are just thoughts you believe to be true. It doesn't make them accurate at all. If you believe them, they become and form your own truth and conception of reality. Only if your mind is open to change can your reality change. So, if you believe you will see Jesus when you die, you will. You will experience exactly what you believed you would. So, the uniqueness that was Terry was still Terry. Her sense of humor remained intact, as she would prove, time and time again. Terry answered many questions… questions we worded to shorten the verbiage in her answering.

I asked her if she had thoroughly believed in God before her death, and she answered, No. I followed with the questions, "Do you believe in God now?" Her answer was "Yes." She said she missed us all and was homesick.

She knew how she died, and she definitely did not want to discuss it. Wherever she was, she told us, there was no one else around and that she never slept nor became tired. Dan asked her if he should sell his car, the one he had while she was still alive, and she answered, "Have a heart."

He then asked if she had anything to say to him, and she replied, "I wuv you." Terry used to do many baby routines to get out of a heated discussion with Dan. She would bring on the baby talk and actions until he dissolved in laughter, wiping their disagreement aside. Finally, she told Dan and me that she was here with us and it was she that told Dan, "I love you" that evening when I walked him to his car.

My husband Don sat in his chair, never saying a word. I asked her if she had a message for her father, and she answered two questions in one as our hands spelled out "Dad, I luv ..." and instead of saying the word "you" as we were expecting, our hands swung around and pointed to Don sitting in his chair. Later Don confided that as I asked Terry the question, his mind wondered how Terry would know which father I was referring to. Her biological father lived in Massachusetts. Don was her stepfather, so she answered his question too.

The evening sped by unnoticed until Dan looked at his watch and saw it was almost three o'clock in the morning. He got up off the floor and said, "I've got to get going, I only have a few hours more until my finals!" Though still resting on the plastic cover, our hands went flying to the word No! on the paper. Dan said he really had to leave and asked if she had any last message for him. All she said was, "I miss you."

It was time to call it a night, and what a night it was! We all said good night to Terry, and I folded up the paper as though mysteriously she was wrapped inside. Dan and his friend left for the dorm; Heather and I went to bed too. Don had gone hours before. The most exciting and meaningful night in my life had come to a close. I saw how the end of our rainbow of life is the start of yet another and far greater one. And religion, any religion is just a means to an end, the end being the beginning of a true search for God.

It was this experience that permanently kept the door to my mind open. I knew, without a doubt, I had experienced Terry, for, with the movement of that little plastic cover, there was a comforting feeling inside. It was one I was to become familiar with as time went on, a growing awareness of knowing something, without knowing how or why.

* * *

Another call to Rose was in order, but I waited for a week before calling. I felt like a child who had eaten half the cookies out of the cookie jar before asking her mother if she could have one. I didn't want to hear what I was doing was wrong, so I put off calling. It was so much fun to know I could talk with Terry anytime I wanted. I didn't want to spoil it, but I finally made the call.

Rose questioned the answers received from Terry. After listening to the answers given, she confirmed that it was Terry and warned me not to use this method much longer and always say a prayer asking for God's help and guidance before beginning. She briefly described from where Terry was communicating to us and how it was possible for other entities to pose as Terry.

Terry could communicate easily now because she was on the astral plane, or what the Catholics would call purgatory. It is in this state that those who die go for rest and adjustment before continuing on. There are, however, those souls on this same plane that may never go any further. They may stay of their own volition, refusing to believe in any more than this, refusing to grow in knowledge and love of God, for the choice is theirs. Hence, there is evil there, and this was no child's play as many used to think and still do. Rose instructed me thoroughly on the procedure and warned me again not to continue for too much longer.

This was extremely difficult for me to accept. I wanted this to go on forever. What a feeling! I could talk to Terry just by putting my hand on this little piece of plastic.

CHAPTER NINE

THE FOLLOWING TWO WEEKS WERE crazy. It was June 14th, and I had to come up with a way to share Terry with her friends. It was something I could not just come right out with and ask, "Hey, how about coming over and chatting with Terry for a while?" They would think I was nuts… and I wouldn't blame them.

So, I called two of Terry's oldest and closest friends, Jennifer and Lori and told them to come over because I had something to show them. When they arrived, they, of course, had no idea what to expect. They followed me into our Florida room, Heather, who was still staying with us, and Terry's friends. Heather was an old pro by this time, and she could hardly wait. We again placed the paper on the floor, covered it with glass, and sat around Indian style. This time though, I said a prayer asking God to allow Terry to talk with us in this manner and asked that no one else come through.

We all placed our fingertips on the small makeup case cover, and I asked if anyone was there. The top vibrated impatiently and whisked our hands to "Yes." Her friends were amazed, and when I asked for the first initial of the person's name and our hands fairly danced to "T." Lori's hand went to her mouth and her eyes filled with tears. She smiled and then yelled, "It's Terry! Oh my God," she cried.

They both tentatively began asking questions, and with every answer, they were more convinced. The questions were those silly, typical, everyday questions they would have asked if Terry was there in the room (as well she was but, in another form). There were no profound inquiries. They had entirely forgotten that she was "dead" and were laughing and talking to her exactly as though she was sitting there with them. They spoke of guys they had dated, who they were dating now, what Terry thought of them, and any other questions that popped into their heads.

They even asked her how many fingers they had held up hiding behind their backs, the color of their underwear, the craziest things you could imagine, and they giggled and laughed with her for hours. They both told Terry how much they loved her, and she told them much the same. She told them she was still homesick, and tears quickly came to my eyes, but the happiness in the air lifted my spirits again, and the conversations continued.

The little get-together lasted for a few hours, and after it was over, they both left far happier than when they arrived. Lori wrote in her diary that night, "At 7:30 PM, I went over to Terry's house. It was the most awesome night in my life. Jennifer, Fran and I, we all talked to Terry. She was really there, she knew what we were doing, what we were wearing, everything! She's not dead. She lives!"

On June 16th, they both returned to continue their conversation in the Florida room while Don chose to stay in the living room and watch television. Again, I prayed that this communication could be and asked for God's protection before we started. It seemed Terry was anxiously awaiting her friends to arrive, for as soon as we placed our hands on the plastic cover, exuberance filled the air, and they began.

I remember suggesting to the girls at one point that we might ask Terry a question of significance or real meaning, considering the circumstances. Both girls looked at me as if to say, "Who cares? We just want to talk with her." So, there was no knowledge gained in this regard. And now I wish I had asked some questions myself, but I was too delirious with happiness to think of it. What was important was that I was talking with Terry, my Terry. I did not give much thought to where she actually was.

The girls asked Terry if they could have one of her gold charms as a remembrance, and she agreed. I went to Terry's jewelry box and brought out all her charms. There were quite a few. The girls made their selections and asked for Terry's okay on the matter. Terry would not give them certain charms, and sometimes they had to make other choices, but finally, both Terry and the girls reached an agreement, and they each had their little charm.

Lori asked Terry if Christopher Wilder was where she was, and Terry replied, "No." That was one of the very few questions we asked relevant to where Terry might be communicating from; all others were just girl talk. Eventually, Don went to bed, and we all moved into the living room to spread out more comfortably on the floor. I felt such peace, but my mind still tried to comprehend how this could possibly be. The girls continued until 5:30 AM. No one remembers now what they talked about or what was said; all they knew was happiness. Their cups had been filled. Looking back on those days, as I now continue my everyday life, I wonder what my friends who saw me on a daily basis, thought of me. They must have thought me very strong and very brave, and at one point, it would have been true. But, unfortunately, right after Terry was killed, my life was hell. There were no little miracles then; there was nothing but emptiness.

Again, only those who have felt this anguish can understand how it feels to pretend to live when your insides are screaming that you really want to die, that you really can't face another thought, another sunrise. How can life dare go on? But I struggled through this period and was never alone. I knew God was with me, and I knew He understood.

I knew, even with all the pain, He was there with love and understanding. Of this, I was sure. This particular aspect of God, however, caught me off guard. Communicating with the deceased was something I had only heard about, but not in a religious vein, and it did not fit into my version of what God and religion were supposed to be like. All these things happened to other people.

Reflecting on what Rose had warned me regarding possibilities of other persons or entities coming through and posing as Terry brought more confusion. I never in my life thought of spirits, good or bad, literally hanging around. Where did they come from? How did they get there, and why were they there? How many people have ever given it a thought? I certainly never had, and I am wondering now what percentage of the population ever has either.

Jennifer and Lori would drop in every now and then as if nothing was unusual about the situation. We simply came back into the Florida room, sat down, and talked. Being aware of the time element, I was unsure how long this could go on and wanted other close friends of Terry to have this experience before something happened, and communication ceased to be.

The first person I thought of was Terry's last boyfriend, Jon, the young man she dated exclusively before Dan. They had been in love for two years, and she had never stopped caring about him, or at least would never wholly give him up. Theirs was a special relationship, but one not meant to be after Dan entered her life. Although they had broken up two years before, they remained very close, and it still infuriated Terry to go out with Dan and find him with another girl.

It was one such encounter that led to a much stranger one after Terry had been killed. Terry and Dan were out dancing at their favorite spot one weekend when they bumped into her old boyfriend and his date. Terry was angry to see Jon with someone else, particularly this one girl. So, she went back out to a nearby convenience store after Dan dropped her off at home. She bought a dozen eggs and drove by the girl's house.

Just as she had expected, Jon's car was parked in the driveway, and they were in the house. It was about two o'clock in the morning when Terry egged his car with the whole dozen eggs. Having had her revenge, she came home and went to bed. When he came out of the house, he was jumping mad! Immediately he knew who did it and he called the next day and gave her hell over the phone. She said he deserved it. Try as I might, I could not make her see how unjustified her actions were.

Three months after Terry's death, I contacted him and asked him to come over to the house because someone here wanted to talk to him. (I had already asked Terry if she would like to, and at first, she said "no," then a week later, she said "yes.") He didn't ask who wanted to talk to him, and I did not volunteer any information.

It was a weekend afternoon, and Lorraine and Heather

were there when he dropped in. Once again, we sat down around the paper on the floor. This time, he asked the questions, knowing he was the only one that knew the answers. He wasn't buying anything. He needed proof. He was there probably one hour, and he, too, knew it was Terry. He asked questions in his mind, not out loud. Lorraine and Heather participated but didn't know the questions.

There was a particular stuffed animal he had given Terry, one that only Terry and he knew the name of, and when asked what it was, she answered immediately. He smiled and said, "Yup, it's Terry, all right!"

He asked her many personal questions that he never shared either the question or the answer to with anyone else. He then confessed to us that he had already "heard" quite explicitly from Terry, and in this conversation, she had confirmed it. A few weeks ago, it seemed that Jon again went out with the same girl who prompted the egging of his car. They had gone out and afterward, had went into her house where he had stayed about an hour. It was past midnight, closer to one in the morning, when Jon left her house. There sat his car, completely covered with pelican droppings! Terry once again had fixed him good, and anyone familiar with pelicans must know that they are very large birds, usually flying four or five in formation, but never at night.

CHAPTER TEN

June was finally coming to an end, and what a month it had been. I kept doing my "writing," trying to identify it. Later, I learned what I was doing was called automatic writing. Some of my messages were from Terry and others from my higher consciousness, my authentic self. Either it was pretty designs, a simple sentence, or simply, "Love, Terry."

By this time, Rose and I had become friends. We had gone through so much together. She had guided me through so very much. Without her answering my questions and giving me a more extensive understanding of God, I do not know at what point I would be in my life right now. A book was constantly in my hands, usually those dealing with psychic phenomena, but I soon lost interest in that phase. Instead, I became more aware of God being the center and my answer to all that had happened and all that would happen.

The word "logic" or "logical" had no more meaning to me whatsoever. If everything in my life had made some sort of sense before, nothing did now, and yet it was happening. It was a fact to me and those who had experienced it with me, but logical? Never. For something to make sense, it had to be understood. It had to be justifiable in my mind. The only thing I knew was that it was Terry and that Terry was still "Terry." Even though I could not see her, death was not death at all.

Why didn't this happen to everybody, or did it? Did it occur to a great many people or just a few, and why? Does everyone who dies try to get in touch with those they left behind? Are we all somehow like radios that are turned off because we have never dared imagine or believe we could hear anything if we learned how to turn ourselves on? If this is so, I want to know why we continue to block our minds entirely to this idea. What could be lost when there is so much to gain? Why fear knowing there is life beyond what we know and levels of knowledge and awareness beyond our wildest dreams? Yes, our everyday life takes all of our time, mere existence absorbs our every waking moment, but when your life shatters with a loss, there is comfort gained in knowing the very person you ache for is always right beside you.

After Terry's death, as I continued writing this story, I realized her death was not a dream because dreams didn't last that long. All of it happened, and there I sat, trying to put my heart and soul on pieces of paper for others to dissect, read, digest, dispense with, or laugh at, and still, the intensity to write was within me. Desperately I wanted those who read this to know the truth, particularly the younger people Terry's age. I wished I could have imparted the basic simplicity of life that I would later learn through her death. We are here because we chose to be here, a choice we made before setting foot on this planet, plain and simple. We are here to be happy, doing what we love to do, and God isn't a distant figure at all but inside each of us. How very much I wished I could have told her, but Terry became my teacher through her death.

It took years for a lot of this knowledge to sink in, and after it did, life became more fascinating than ever!

Is there a chance of convincing someone of something they have never believed in? Could I, or anyone else, make someone's mind crank open when it is so easy to keep it shut with the written word? Why on earth bother? What excited me does not necessarily throw everyone else into a frenzy, and yet, oh, how I want to share my feelings. That sensation of "knowing" something so extraordinary, so wonderful, it has to get out of my insides and somehow spread to others. In advertisements for perfumes in magazines, they sometimes have a small square to "scratch and sniff" to enable you to know what the scent smells like. How I wish it could be so with feelings. We are inept at describing the essential things in our lives, the knowledge that sets us free.

Many believe that the friends of Jesus Christ experienced Him after death. They had seen and talked with Him. They had no doubt. I did not see Terry, but if I had not personally experienced the events I have written and those to follow, I would have kept on in my everyday ordinary life as best I could under the circumstances. In my heart and in my mind, there is no doubt that my daughter loved and did love her friends and me enough to bring about the things that happened. If there were any doubt in my mind, I would not dare put this down on paper, much less tell anyone outside my immediate family about it. Terry was calling the shots, this is her story, through me, and it has to be told. Once told, the book itself may be closed. The story will continue.

After checking with other people, one of Terry's friends became convinced that the Ouija board was evil. I later realized that this was the only way Terry could figure out how to get in touch with all of us. When people have died, they all have their own ways to attempt reaching us: a song, a bird, a scent, so many, many ways they try to comfort us, and if we're not aware, we miss the gift.

* * *

The friend who questioned the gift has my compassion because those who have died don't send letters or use the telephone to make contact. (I did know a friend who received a call at three in the morning from her deceased sister who had an unresolved issue. I always wondered what the charges on that call would be!)

There was a handful of us involved in this bizarre incident. Was it a coincidence that it only happened to those Terry truly loved with her whole heart while still alive? No, it was God's loving way to allow a handful of people to know that their heartache should not be and that Terry did exist in another state and was not dead. That time of communicating with her fades quickly, and it will not continue much longer. She was at a point where she could do this. Soon, she will be there no longer. My prayer was that her friend, who doubted, ask herself if it was joy that Terry gave her and be grateful to receive this last beautiful gift.

Maybe God wants us to keep an open mind. If we have never asked ourselves, "What if this could be?" Then we will never know the answers to anything and will search for other's truths until we find their answers. I would suggest that we find our own. To turn the sunshine and joy Terry brought to us into rain and say it is not God's doing makes my heart weep. Must we always seek others' approval for our own experiences? If some of you would only dare to say to yourself, "What if?" after someone you loved has died, I believe many of you would be astounded to find the voices in your head to be those who left you behind. If you were to listen to those voices, there would be cheering in heaven because you had the courage to dare, and for those trying desperately to assure you they still were in existence but just simply out of your sight, there would be happiness.

* * *

There was a small amount of money donated in Terry's memory. I had never found a place for it, and almost a year after Terry's death, I had asked Terry's friend, the same one that doubted she had talked with her, what she thought Terry would do with the money. "Terry would divide it among her friends or buy them each something with it," was her reply. There wasn't much there, but Terry would have blown every cent on her friends and us, I was sure. The thought stayed with me for a day or two. I wanted something done with the money, something in her name.

Maybe I should divide it among her friends, I thought, but that just didn't seem right to me for some reason. Then it hit me. Terry had already given her gift to her friends, everyone she could. Some took this gift, the proof of her existence, after her so-called death, with love and appreciation; others questioned its worth and even its truth. She had given the most priceless of gifts. She could give no more. After reading many books, I had learned many things. One was that the friends of Terry who experienced her after she died were chosen in some way beyond my knowledge for their own spiritual growth and development. It was not by chance that these few had this opportunity. Terry's gift knew no price, and what a heavenly gift it was!

I had a lot of thoughts about God. New thoughts. We have heard that God is always with us, and assuming this to be true, we, too, are all a part of this same God. How do we find that part of us and become familiar with it? It doesn't sound easy, nor does it sound too complicated, but how do we find the God within us when we don't fully comprehend who we are? It is a trip in itself and one I am presently on. It is the birth of free thought within me, unencumbered by beliefs planted and accepted unquestionably since my very own beginning. While thinking of beliefs, I realized most of us accept our parent's beliefs and make them our own, whether it be religion, politics, etc. What if our parents were wrong? We would then be simply assimilating their truth and their errors. The absolute truth might lie somewhere waiting for you to discover.

This journey to finding ourselves is taken slowly, a journey into oneself, like a boxer taking little jabs at his opponent before creating an opening and plowing in full force. Testing my strengths is enjoyable, for I am only too quick to go on about my good points. My faults are frankly painful and uncomfortable to bring out into the daylight. It's easier to keep them hidden, surrounded by my more favorable parts. But if we also know that our authentic selves are indeed perfect and that which we see as imperfect is only the fabrications our minds come up with from the beliefs we hold on to. Beliefs change with knowledge; knowledge changes with new beliefs.

It is a journey in which we come face to face with our true selves for the very first time. We will see the culmination of all we have been and all we have ever believed in. It is made manifest in us. The light dawns when we are aware that we create our own world with our own thoughts and beliefs, and with this knowledge comes our freedom. When this glorious dawning occurs, when we know that we, too, are creators, when we know without a doubt what our reason for living is and how and why we chose how our lives will be, God smiles. The doors of heaven are flung open.

CHAPTER ELEVEN

It was now August, and in the back of my mind, off in the corner, sat a timer. Soon the time would run out, and there would be no more talking with Terry. How I hated the thought of this. It was so important to me that everyone who should talk with Terry in this way does so. Only one person came to mind, a secret admirer at the time of her death and a very special person to Terry. Part of the rewards of being close to someone are the little secrets shared, and Terry and I had shared many. Here was one such secret.

It had started when Terry worked at a tee-shirt designing and manufacturing company. She was one of the first employees hired when the company first started, and there were just a few employees. One young man was the head artist and a part owner in the company. He was just twenty-four years old, a quiet and sensitive man. Somehow though, quiet as he was, they hit it off because they both shared the same sense of humor.

Terry told me that this young man made her day by walking by and saying a few words to her when she was disgruntled at her job. If, for some reason, he failed to see her, she said her day was flat. Humor is such an excellent tonic! Their friendship at work grew. Both of them were dating others, so they were relatively safe in their harmless flirting. Or so they thought. Kiddingly, one day I remarked to Terry that she should watch the relationship because sharing laughter was an excellent prerequisite for love.

She just grinned at me and went on to tell me he was just ordinary-looking and that I would meet him someday and just know without being introduced, know who he was. She often mentioned his sense of humor and said I would love it, but nothing was funny about anything when I finally met him.

Terry had many so-called "loves." For example, if we were driving somewhere and she spotted a very handsome young man, she would look at him dreamingly and say, "I'm in love." That was one of her favorite expressions, and I don't know how many times I had heard it from her and would chuckle every time I did.

Once, the day before Valentine's Day, she came bursting into the kitchen after work to show me a card the friend at work had given her. On the outside of the card was a giant green olive, and on the inside was printed, "Olive you," signed by him. Terry just loved the card and was so thrilled, and wanted to do something to reciprocate. It just so happened that we had an enormous fake green olive in the house that would fill a glass by itself.

I had bought it many years ago as a joke and put it in Don's martini. I never threw it out. It just moved from drawer to drawer in the kitchen over the years. Terry asked if she could have it, and the following day at work, she placed the olive in his car with the word "too" written on a piece of paper attached to it. She was very pleased with herself and the whole little business with the olive, but that was all there was to that. Life went on as usual. They both continued to date whomever they were dating but enjoyed each other's company and humor at work.

When Terry was missing, and I was half crazy with worry, doing anything to keep busy, I drove over to where she worked to see their new building and just to be close to the things and place that Terry was close to. Entering the lobby, I gave my name to the receptionist and asked to see the particular man Terry always talked about. After waiting a few minutes, three men came into the area at once from different directions, but I walked directly to him and put out my hand, and introduced myself.

"How did you know it was me?" he asked, and I remembered Terry's words to me just a few months before. She was right. I knew him right off the bat. There wasn't much to talk about, but it was a pleasure to meet him. He was very personable, and everything Terry had said he would be.

When the news came about Terry, all of her co-workers at the tee shirt company were all heart- broken, so the company dedicated their next two-page advertisement in a national magazine to her. She would have been thrilled and proud of it. An ad was drawn up composed of two pictures of Terry on a filmstrip running diagonally across both pages at an angle. In the lower right-hand corner of the page laid a single red rose. Under the rose was written, "In memory of Terry Ferguson, a dedicated employee and an upcoming model until her untimely death. She'll always be remembered for being truly World Class."

Most people would not even notice an olive tucked under the foliage of the rose or understand its significance.

And if the advertisement, held in a certain light at a certain angle, an inscription would be seen under her photograph, "Olive you," with his signature. So, keeping this in mind, it only seemed natural that I would invite him over.

This particular night was neither long nor involved. There was not the strong communication as before. I just hoped something would happen for him. He had cared for her deeply. We began as I had many times before. It felt like we were picking up a signal as a receiver would, but the transmitter was not strong enough. Finally, after giving her initial "T," two simple words followed. They were "Olive you." We were both satisfied with who the message came from, making him feel so much better. I felt I had fulfilled my mental list of people with whom Terry would have chosen to make contact. Now all I could do was watch helplessly as the time ran out.

That evening after he left, we got a telephone call from a close family friend who had moved to Arkansas after Terry's death. He called to tell me of a strange incident that had just happened to him that afternoon. Before he even began to tell me, I knew what he was going to talk about because he and Terry went back years. He was the one who took the first professional pictures of Terry when she was twelve years old and found so much potential in the resulting photographs.

He had watched her grow from a child to a woman, and they were very close. She jokingly called him "uncle," teasing him to make him feel older. The day he called, he had gone fishing, and while peacefully waiting for a nod from his fishing pole, his thoughts turned to Terry. Suddenly out of the corner of his eye, something caught his attention up on the cliff overlooking the river. There, stood Terry smiling down at him and in the next instant—nothing. He was so moved, he came right home and wrote a poem about her, then called us and shared what he wrote.

For Terry

I knew her as a child and as a young girl,
And then, to my surprise, a young woman.
What wonder, what excitement to everyone
She touched.
I was one of the lucky ones,
I knew her beauty,
I knew her smile …
She kissed me once, and a joy
I had never felt consumed me.
She was a spirit, I thought, that would
Be part of everyone she embraced.
I still see her as if it were now, I
Know her presence, her immense love of life.
There is no loneliness when I think of her,
For she is with me, as with all of us.

Had this been the first such incident, I would have had mixed emotions, but I knew something different was going on by this time, and I had no problem convincing him that I believed his story wholeheartedly. Just a few days before, Terry's girlfriend, Jennifer froze while was dancing at one of their favorite nightspots. Watching her from across the room, wearing the same dress they had shopped for together, stood Terry, smiling at her, then nothing. Gone.

Her friend went to a psychiatrist and was told it was simply a trick of her mind due to the shock of her loss. I wonder how many of her other friends had fleeting incidents swept away as imaginative thoughts during this time. What a shame. This was the same friend who talked with Terry for hours through the Ouija board and later declared that it had to be the work of the devil since it was impossible.

Days passed that found me wrapped in my very own

personal grief. After my husband left for work each morning, forgetting all the good things that had happened to me, I would again feel the loss, the betrayal, and the anger at her death. It just wasn't enough for me to know that she was in existence in another state. My selfishness shone through, but I wouldn't call it that. I called it grieving. That was more acceptable to me.

Conversations between Rose and me drifted back. I could hear Rose telling me that Terry chose this path to her death. It sounded so ludicrous, so far-fetched when I heard it. I didn't believe it. Now I do. Rose had told me that eleven months before Terry died, she made a big choice, one that led her to this nightmare. Even the newspapers wrote that it seemed destiny played the leading role in this tragedy. One coincidence after another led Terry to Christopher Wilder, and there was no mistake in that.

Sorting through her things, months later, I found a letter that Terry never mailed to her boyfriend, Dan, written exactly eleven months before being killed. In the letter, Terry told Dan that she had finally decided that she would achieve her goal through modeling, no matter what. Terry only asked for his patience and support. It was something she had to do.

Our home was still full of the feeling of Terry. Whether or not she was here all the time or a part of it, the sense was strong. It may have been this feeling of her being around so much that made me miss her physical self even more. I could talk to her and, in some instances, hear her reply, especially when I would be having a good cry. She would give me hell. Little things continued to occur so I would have my proof and not doubt my sanity any more than I did. These little things, as I called them, always happened when I was least expecting anything; that's when she would dazzle me with her little love signs and signals.

Engrossed in yard work one morning, she chose to drop

in and let me know I was on her mind. Mowing the lawn was one of my favorite things to do, even in the hot Florida sun. It's good to feel the heat, feel the physical exercise, look around after finishing and find everything looking neat and beautiful. But my mind was somewhere else as I mowed strip after strip, checking all the time to see if I missed a blade of grass here or there. Finally, I stopped the mower to empty the full grass catcher bag into a barrel. As I took the grass catcher bag off of the mower, it was as though I had put my head into a vast oven filled with just-baked chocolate chip cookies. The delicious smell was overpowering. There I stood, encased in their aroma. Then as quickly as it happened, the scent dissipated. Terry's favorite food was chocolate, her favorite cookie, chocolate chip. All I could do was cry, but my tears were happy tears sweetened by her touch.

Another morning, after Don had left for the golf course, Terry paid me another visit. Breakfast was over; I had placed the dishes in the dishwasher and cleaned off the counter. There were two pieces of bacon left, sitting on a piece of paper towel that I couldn't figure out what to do with. I left them sitting there and went back to the bedroom to make the bed. That done, I wandered back to the kitchen.

Placed as before on the counter on a paper towel were the two strips of bacon sitting on the floor exactly square to the bottom of the counter. They couldn't have just fallen. They looked as though someone had carefully placed them there. Then it hit me, and I smiled, "Good morning Terry."

I started to make note of all these little things. When a blue mood began to creep in, I would look at the growing list and think of God and how great His love had been to me. There is a list of people who experienced Terry in and out of this house. A list of names is just that. The important thing is "So what!" If these people forget and chalk it up to something other than what it was, it becomes their loss. Among her friends and acquaintances, whoever was aware of her presence, were given it for a purpose, especially for them and no one else. God opened their minds and hearts. My prayer is they are never closed again. That is up to them.

We gently ignored upcoming family birthdays and holidays. Instead, Don and I acknowledged the occasions. There was no need in pretending special days did not come up, but we just let them go as quietly as they came. Previously we always had our small family traditions that now seemed stupid without Terry.

Now, my birthday was approaching, my first without her. In the past, Don would give Terry money so she could shop for him. It worked out great because, like most young women, Terry loved to shop and was an excellent shopper. She had an eye for quality and class, but she had an eye for a sale too, and she prided herself for saving money whenever she went on a spree.

Usually, there would be the whispering in the back bedroom when Don gave her the money. Sometimes she would come back in a few hours, collect more money from him and flit out the door again. This year, Don was on his own, but I took him off the hook, did my own shopping for my birthday present, and took Terry with me. It sounds crazy to some, or maybe to most, but we had a good time to those that understand.

In one particular instance, while in a dressing room, I could not figure out what was the matter with the dress I was trying on. It just looked wrong, and I didn't know why. The dress was gauze, in teal blue, with a V-neck and four large buttons down the back. As I stood looking puzzled at my reflection in the mirror, I heard,

"Mum, for God's sake, you've got the dress on backwards!" Sure enough, the buttons were in the front, not the back, and

I could hear Terry laughing. After buying the dress, I went to the shoe store across the street to find a pair of shoes that would go with it. It took some poking around, but I finally came up with two pairs I really loved and couldn't decide between them when Terry piped in again, "Oh ma, buy both of them for heaven's sake!" and I did.

The week proceeding my birthday and a few days afterward, were very special for me. There was no missing Terry, no sadness. Instead, I was enfolded entirely in a sensation of incredible peace, warmth, and love. This feeling engulfed me and held me so tenderly I felt nothing in the world could hurt or bother me. I was joyously invincible. Rose called this a "Love Wave" from Terry, and it was a good description because it hit me like a big soft wave and held me with the feeling of buoyancy in an ocean of love for days and days. I had experienced sublime tranquility. Yet, with every experience encountered, more were waiting. I became a seeker, actively pursuing the truth about God that had never entered my mind before. All my questions and answers returned to God as their source. All the things that had happened to me, Terry's friends, and Terry herself were through God. Simplicity is often difficult to comprehend.

As I continued to read and study, delving now more into the conscious and sub-consciousness of man, I realized I was exploring the biggest mystery of them all, and what a thriller!

My wanderings throughout the house inevitably took me into Terry's room. It remained the same as she had left it, except for the clothes my niece took back with her after the funeral. Her junk still permeated the room, and I would try to throw things out, I mean, really try. Every damn thing in that room screamed her name, her feelings, and her memories. Try as I might, I ended up putting back her silly things on her dresser or her desk and just walking out. So much for my inner strength.

When I tried to push myself, it was always worse. Gradually the strength would come that would enable me to throw out a simple pack of matches bearing the name of the last restaurant she and Dan had gone to, theatre tickets torn in half--all pieces of her life. But, dear God, to throw them away was as if I were throwing her away and that I could never do. Where was the line drawn, though? It seemed this was some sort of a test, and I knew I was failing miserably.

Sandwiched into the summer months was a vacation trip with friends to the mountains of the Carolinas. It seemed like a great idea at the time, but evidently, I was not ready for it at all. Instead of relaxing, I felt the pressure of being forced to. It was as though I was to be kept busy and happy all the time, like a child in camp, and I wanted neither. My idea of a great time was a good book, peace, and quiet, but that didn't seem to be on the schedule.

* * *

Now, looking back, I know I was feeling sorry for myself. There was no way I was going to have a good time, no matter what. I was lousy vacation material. These friends were good friends, and I had shared my secret "writings" with them, but they were undoubtedly uncomfortable if I had a paper and pen in front of me. Who could blame them? I know my girlfriend's husband thought I was losing it or had already lost it. My girlfriend understood.

Writing objectively now is easy. I am not the same person I was then, nor will I be tomorrow. None of us are. We are ever-changing beings. On that vacation, I was on my own trip, my own little trip of misery. I felt nothing inside me, and I wanted only to be alone. In suffering from a loss, only you know when you need a break from it. A forced respite by someone else brings a worthless reprieve in the hurting.

Knowing when you are ready is the hard part. It still seemed that the closer I was to familiar surroundings, the closer I was in thought to God and Terry. So, escape itself was impossible. Maybe it was unnecessary. The reckoning, the balance between living this life now and placement of Terry within it, seems my daily quandary. Knowing the choice between being happy and miserable is mine, and mine alone gives me no one to blame for how I feel except myself.

There were enough things to bring pain into my life that surrounded Terry's disappearance and death. They faded away slowly. The difficulty was in making sure I was not indeed looking for them. We can bring about any emotion we desire if we decide to, and truthfully, they can sneak in if we are unaware of it. Many times, I just let it happen and had a damn good cry. The hurt and pain do build up sometimes, but that's okay. That's only normal. The trick is how to let the pain go and get on with life.

I was told the pain that feels as though someone is scraping out the inside of your heart with a dull knife would begin lessening after a few months. That was a blessing. The dull ache that replaced it was easier to bear. The only way to take life was moment to moment. Then, when thoughts strayed to even one memory, my heart would take a painful plunge again.

Many sleepless nights saw me walking from room to room, looking out the windows, roaming like a spirit myself. Sleep was elusive, and I was ever on its trail throughout the house. I would often catch it in the guest bedroom and drift off into its dreams, hoping this one would be the one I would awaken from and find Terry's car parked outside again. But this night held something better than dreams. I didn't have the faintest idea how it happened at the time and how Terry was a part of it. I just knew it happened and that I will never forget it.

Sleep came to me, and I drifted off. The very next thing I knew, I saw myself "come out of myself," lying on the bed. That's not exactly true. I could not see "me." I just knew I was looking down at what I believed to be me on the bed, sleeping. There is no recollection of myself as me from my vantage point, but I knew it was me bobbing on the bedroom ceiling and loving the feeling. It was fantastic! It was me, and I was completely weightless though I could feel a slight sensation of my body against the ceiling.

Luckily, I had read some books on the subject and knew what was going on. I just wasn't prepared for it. I had tried this a few times before, but each attempt failed, so I just gave it up. So now, without even thinking, here I was! The name of this is astral projection. Briefly, it is the sensation of observing phenomena from a perspective that does not coincide with the physical body. Usually, a silver thread or cord connects your physical body to the astral body, but I saw nothing. I was too excited to be very observant.

Imagine waking up some night as I did and ending up on the ceiling looking down at yourself! Well, there I was, and I wanted to make the most of it while it lasted, so I thought of drifting into our bedroom since I was still in the guest bedroom and peek in on Don. As I thought that, I realized I was directly over the bed I was sleeping in, and it looked like quite a distance down to the mattress itself. What if I were to fall? Immediately, as if I was on an elevator, my "body" began to descend toward the bed gently. As I was about a foot and a half away, I was dropped face-first into the pillow with a plop! At that instant, my head hit the pillow; I heard Terry's laughter and giggle so loud I woke up, sitting bolt upright in bed. How Terry entered into this experience, I didn't know at the time. Was she a bystander to my little trip to nowhere, or did she in some way help bring it about? Humor-wise, it was right up her alley and something she would do if given a chance. Although the event itself is nothing unheard of, nor is it something that hasn't happened many times before to different people, it certainly was new to me! I had never heard of anyone mentioning anything like that before, but why would they anyway? Frankly, I would have wondered about them had I heard such a tale before reading about it myself.

At least I could talk to Rose and my best friend, Lorraine, about my happy experiences, this one in particular. Some of my other friends probably thought I was going a little nuts after hearing some of my stories; why give them more fuel for the fire? I learned to keep my mouth shut. It was no easy feat for me at first, but I had learned my lesson. Now I'm putting it all down on paper for everyone to read anyway. Why let only a few know when everyone can know? It doesn't make much sense viewing it that way, but I know I'm not crazy, and that's all that matters to me. I know others have gone through many of these same things and have not dared talk about it for many of the same reasons.

Some of the things that happened to me made me think of the letter I had received from the mother of a murdered girl. This woman had suffered the same pain as I had, but I wondered if I could have survived the pain as well as I did without the little "extras" from Terry. I had been given proof. Would I have made it through the nightmare without it? My faith is unshakable, so I would have, but why do these things happen to some and not others? Do they happen, and people are not even aware of them?

There is one family I know of that it did happen to. They called me to tell me about what they were experiencing, not knowing I was going through the same thing. It was the family of a seventeen-year-old girl struck by lightning at the beach. I had sent a sympathy card to the family after reading about it in the local paper. The girl reminded me of a younger Terry, and from what I read, she was the perfect teenager who had everything going for her. So, when I sent them the card, I let them know I had experienced a similar loss and felt deeply sorry for them.

The dead girl's brother called me a few days afterward to thank me for the card. He spoke for his parents, whose command of the English language was not very good, but the words said the same in any language. We talked about his sister, Maria, and Terry, and he brought up how very upset his sister was over Terry's death. She, too, had aspirations to be a model. Then he went on to tell me, unprompted, that some funny things had occurred. The day Maria went to the beach and was killed, she cleaned her room, putting everything back in order, entirely unlike her. She then put her crucifix on an existing chain because the original chain had broken and put it on her neck. The last thing she did was beg her mother to borrow her wedding band just this once so she could wear it.

Her mother obliged.

The family was at the beach when a sudden lightning storm approached, and everyone headed for the shore. Unfortunately, a bolt of lightning killed her instantly while leaving the water's edge. The last things she saw were the faces of her brother, sister, and her mother. Surrounded by the faces of those she loved, she was gone.

That night, he told me that something strange occurred when consoling his mother in his sister's bedroom. Night had crept in while they both sat on her bed. So deep were they in their grief there was no sense of light or dark. Suddenly they both snapped out of it. There was a sound of movement on the other side of the bed.

They both turned to see a figure with dark hair, clothed

entirely in a long white robe, move from the bed and disappear after a few steps into forever. They were positive it was Maria. It gave them a great sensation of peace. How many such stories are there? It was a fluke that I heard that one. I can't help but wonder if that was their only experience or if there were others, but they moved away shortly afterward, so I'll never know.

CHAPTER TWELVE

IN SEPTEMBER, DON AND I flew to Cape Cod, Massachusetts, for ten days, and I loved every minute. This was home to me, my other home. Although I loved Florida, part of me will always remain in my hometown of Falmouth. I spent most of my growing up years in this town and enjoyed a storybook life. I had married Terry's father here, and although the marriage was short-lived, there were no regrets or bad feelings when we divorced. Terry was born in the neighboring town of Hyannis and, after we moved to Florida, would always return to the Cape when she had a vacation. She loved it. Small New England towns are unique in their simplicity and charm. Falmouth was such a town, sitting overlooking the Atlantic Ocean and hosting thousands of tourists in the summer months. The best time to visit Cape Cod is in Indian summer after everyone has left. There you can find its peace and beauty, laced with the salty air, and know privacy at the same time. Choosing September as we did, gave us un-crowded streets, empty beaches, and best of all, perfect weather.

Tucked into my luggage was my little plastic makeup cover and paper. I had some hope of having my family contact Terry, though Rose told me she thought it would be doubtful, but I could try. Terry's presence accompanied us on the plane trip to Massachusetts, so I kept on hoping. Arriving at Logan International Airport in Boston, I felt Wilder had soiled the place by his previous presence here and was aware of his passage through this very same terminal on his way to New Hampshire and his death. I forgot these thoughts when we saw the faces of my sister and brother-in-law. After fighting our way through traffic, we were on Route 28, the way "home."

Mom and dad had found us a cottage to stay in to be alone and have some privacy. It was kitty-corner to my parent's house and was one that had enchanted me all through my growing-up years. Nestled in among large old oak trees, sitting back quietly, it always reminded me of Snow White's house and still does. Flagstones paced themselves to the front door in dainty steps, and a large flat mass of stone, semi-level, introduced you to the front door. Once inside, it was typical of all summer cottages with their knotty pine walls, hardwood floors, and a fireplace. Childhood fantasies and dreams issue from every timber in this little cottage. It felt as though this house was steeped in love, and the love continued to linger on and on.

How funny to fall in love with a structure, but this house entranced me. It was an instant home. Mornings, I would awake to the sounds of gulls screaming. One particular night I woke to my favorite sound, the foghorn, with its wonderful old haunting and heart-rending notes drifting off the ocean and into the coastal area, caressing everything in its path with its moist touch. Sometimes, it seemed when the ocean had had so much to say, it would have to use the foghorn to interpret its feeling, and the foghorn cooperated, never letting its friend down. It is as if the ocean bares its soul when the foghorn's sound permeates the night.

The first night on the Cape, we ate dinner at mom and dad's. It was so good to sit down with my parents again and enjoy both the meal and the light conversation. After dinner, I got up and wandered into the living room. Everything looked like an ad out of "House Beautiful," the cheery fireplace, the Kennedy rocking chair, the braided rugs on the floor…all said, "Welcome home." Her living room walls were full of all my oil paintings done throughout the years. One caught my eye, and I groaned out loud at how awful it was.

Mom heard me and came into the room and asked what I was muttering about. I pointed to the one painting of mine and said, "Mom, please take that terrible thing down." It was one of my first paintings, and boy did it ever smack of it. I cringed just to look at it. Mom liked it because it was one of my very first, and as much as I begged, she would not renege. I even offered to paint another to take its place—no luck. For the rest of the evening, I kept bringing up the picture, but Mom was firm. The painting would stay.

The following day the problem of the picture had been resolved by Terry, and I laughed myself silly over it.

"Francie, the darndest thing happened last night after you left, and we went to bed." Sometime in the middle of the night, she heard a sound from the living room and, being too tired to check it out, just rolled back over and went back to sleep. Mom woke in the morning and checked on the cause of the noise. The painting I had complained about was on the floor. Mom couldn't hang it back up because the frame had broken.

"I told you I didn't like the painting, mom," I laughed, "Terry just helped me, that's all."

We were not having any luck reaching Terry with the paper we used as our Ouija board, but her humor and presence were felt. There was no doubt that she was around.

A few nights later, mom was reading in the kitchen at the breakfast table. A small table lamp sat in the middle and was used when the overhead light was switched off. Dad had preceded mom to bed, and as was his habit, he locked the kitchen door and turned off the overhead light by turning the small knob at its base. Mom read for a while, and her mind began to drift.

Putting the book aside, mom talked to Terry in her mind, telling her how much she loved and missed her, and wondered if she was around or if she could hear her. Within minutes, the light overhead clicked on. Mom sat transfixed in the light for a few seconds. She then realized who had dropped by to let her know she was listening and was indeed around. This light had never done this before, nor has it since. Mom did not doubt that Terry wanted her to know she was there and put any doubts aside. I could not fathom how these physical things could be in my wildest imagination, but later with Rose's teachings, I would understand completely.

Terry was also close to my younger sister, and she had heard from Terry quite a few times. The messages she received were almost verbatim to what Rose had told me Terry had communicated to her. I never realized it until months later when I re-read my sister's letters and saw in amazement both my sister and Rose had said the same thing! My sister and Terry had spent many years in close association as small children. Though Terry moved to Florida, whenever she came to the Cape for the summer or a visit, she always squeezed in time to spend with my sister, even if it was just a shopping trip to Boston. My younger sister was only four years Terry's senior and would be kiddingly called "Auntie" by Terry. They were different in many ways, but they didn't grow up like relatives; they grew up the best of friends despite these differences.

While we were on the Cape, my Aunt Myra and Uncle John came down from New Hampshire to see us. Those two people were extremely special to me. Both were artists. Myra painted her dreams and visions in oil, and John carved miracles from wood. They had lost their thirty-year-old daughter, Vicky, four years before from a rare blood disorder, and they shared my pain and loss of Terry.

At the time, we were all gathered at mom's house. It was a mini-family reunion, and everyone was talking at once, bringing up old family jokes and reliving old memories. It was great. During the conversation I had alone with Myra, she told me that she had been plagued with her daughter's last words that I had been unaware of all these years.

As she held Vicky's hand when she lay in her hospital bed, Vicky said, "Momma, I'm in hell." She never regained consciousness, and Myra carried those painful words in her heart, knowing her daughter had died an unhappy death. When she told me, I excused both Myra and myself from the group and literally dragged her across the street to our little cottage. I just had to do something. Maybe I could contact Vicky! I had the feeling it was right. We went into the house and sat down at the kitchen table. I placed the paper and plastic top in front of us while Myra looked questioningly at me. I just told her to try something with me for a minute. She was very nervous but put her fingers lightly on the plastic and tried to relax. I then asked if there was anyone there that would like to talk to us. Our fingers were sliding easily to "yes," and when I asked if it was someone we both knew, the reply was "yes" again. Just as I was in the process of asking the next question, both of Myra's hands dropped like a stone to her sides. Tears welled in her eyes. I didn't know what was going on and asked, "What's the matter? What happened?" She answered a little shakily, "I just heard Vicky's voice as plain as I hear you. She just said, "Mom, I love you." We did not go any further. There was no need. We didn't speak about this to anyone when we joined the others. Later, I received a note from Myra telling me that that incident stopped the pain and brought her peace for the first time since Vicky's death.

A purpose served, but it was not by me. I was like a waitress bringing an excellent meal to the table. God did the cooking, so all compliments belonged to the chef. God worked a miracle, and I somehow was the one chosen to carry it to a hungering customer. I do not know why this happened, but I was overwhelmed with happiness and gratitude to be a part of anything that helped take the hurt away.

When I first wrote this, almost a year later, I thought of Vicky's tormented last words, "Momma, I'm in hell." They may well have been her sorrowful way of conveying to her mother the fact that this life she had lived on this earth had indeed been her hell, and though sorry for the pain she caused by leaving, she had earned her peace and happiness and was eager to go. She just wanted her mother to understand.

We had a great vacation. The weather remained picture-perfect every day. My sister and brother-in-law put on a clambake for us to top it all off before we left. After an eventful vacation, we were finally homeward bound, and I was already looking forward to hearing from Rose. She had said she would have a seminar dealing with some of the things I was questioning, and I could hardly wait. But before the workshop happened, there was another major surprise or reward for what I could only assume was my faith.

CHAPTER THIRTEEN

IT WAS THE NIGHT OF October 1st. Dan had come over for dinner, and it was a particularly fun-filled evening. We were all in high spirits. When it came time for Dan to go, I walked him to his car and waved goodbye as he drove out of sight. It always seemed when he drove off that Terry was there, sitting beside him. I bet she was. As if in some kind of cruel punishment, whenever I had an especially happy time, shortly afterward, I hit a new low. The pain crept in, and missing her hit me cruelly that night. After Dan left, my husband wanted to watch a particular television show and I another. I went into Terry's room and watched her small, black and white. I propped my feet on her desk and watched the show I wanted to see, then joined Don in the living room a half-hour later. It was ten o'clock by now. Don and I talked a little while, and he went on to bed. I said I'd be in shortly, but I knew inside me, it would be quite a while. I needed a good, hard cry. Rarely did I ever fall apart unless I was alone. It seemed a personal grief, strictly between Terry and me. I shared it with no one else except God. My insides hurt so much, even after crying. I wandered to the guest bedroom that looked out at the front of the house. My eyes went to where her car always used to be parked. The thought was always present that this was just an awful dream, and I would wake up. God, how I missed her! The worst part of the pain was easing, but the loneliness and the missing never stopped.

Looking out the front window that night, fully realizing that I had actually talked with Terry and had proof given to me that she still "was," I still at that moment felt such a need, such a longing for her, I begged God with all my heart to let me know by some sign that she was happy and okay because I loved her so much. With that prayer, I finally went to bed.

The next morning, after a good night's sleep and never missing the absence of hurt, I sat with Don reading the morning paper. He went off to work as usual, and I started my routine of housework as the morning moved on. For some reason, I went into Terry's room, spotted the chair where I left it the night before and was going to push it under the desk, but something was on it. I had been sitting on this chair the night before; now, there was a little pile of powder about one inch high, right in the middle. It appeared to be some sort of face powder. If only words could describe what I felt, "astounded" is close, but it still didn't touch it. Leaning over Terry's chair, I caught my reflection in the mirror but had to look closer. There was fresh powder on her mirror too! It looked as though someone had dipped a hand in water, then heavily into powder, and then flicked it directly onto its surface.

Tears streamed down my face. Here was my answer

to the prayer I had so pleaded for. Here was my proof I could see, feel and touch. I wasn't losing my mind either! All I could do was thank God for loving me so much. When my euphoria passed, I started double-checking around the room for another source of the powder. Could it be dust that had fallen from the ceiling? No, that was out. Was there face powder in her desk drawer that somehow got on her chair? No, there was none around. In fact, there wasn't any more in the house. I had thrown it all out. I looked at the flicked-on powder on the makeup mirror on her desk. It dispelled any doubts. There was no explanation. There was no explaining away anything. Can anyone explain God?

Months later, thinking about this, I checked my calendar for October 1st to see if there was any significance, date-wise. Terry's birthday was October eighth, so that wasn't it. Then, however, my Catholic calendar handed me another jolt. October 1st was the Feast of St. Theresa of the Roses, called the Little Flower. I had been so taken by the statue of this dark-haired beauty with roses in her hands when I was a child that it was she I chose to name my daughter after. Coincidence? I really don't know, but maybe someday.

Don came home for lunch, and though knowing he preferred not to be made aware of all these things and was tired of all the writings and happenings, I was determined this was not to be ignored. "Honey, come into Terry's room for a minute; I want to show you something," I managed nonchalantly. Picking up the hidden tone in my voice, he begrudgingly stepped into her room. I showed him the powder on her chair and mirror, having already explained my prayer of the night before. I turned to him and asked, "Okay, so where did it come from?" "Well, there has to be a scientific explanation for all this, that's all," he said. To him, it just was not possible, that simple!

Yet another reason I am positive God has a terrific sense

of humor when he created us, for love and laughter do, after all, go hand in hand. Eventually, I put the mirror on the top shelf of Terry's closet so the powder would be untouched. Although I never touched the powder nor sat in that chair, it eventually went away. I thought of having the powder analyzed, but I didn't care what it contained or didn't contain. I knew that powder was put there by either a higher source than I had ever encountered, or my daughter put it there to stop me from hurting. Either way, it was through God. If I didn't know any better, I would have called it a miracle, but it certainly didn't impress anybody I showed it to. Then again, they probably thought I put it there. I can't blame them. I would have probably thought the same thing if all this had happened to one of my friends. Until you have been there, you just do not know what it is like. Since Terry's death, my utmost efforts are those that deal with keeping my mouth shut when it comes to criticism of someone else. One way or another, judgment, meted out by God, most assuredly does not need my expertise.

Of course, I called Rose called right away. My insides were shouting with joy, and it had to be shared. She expressed her delight and happiness for me, and we firmed up plans for the upcoming seminar only days away.

Lorraine stayed with me the weekend of the seminar. We were like two little children gaining entrance to a free candy shop, and we tried to digest everything. There was much food for thought, too, the meaning of words unfamiliar to me— auras, telekinesis, past life regression, and karma, to name a few. There was no mystery to any of it. It all made sense. The secret lies in knowing what these things meant. We all took part in experiments that fascinated us by their simplicity, but what was more remarkable was to learn of all the abilities we never dreamed we had. We were all doing things we had never done before because we didn't know we knew how to do them. It reminded me of my earlier painting lessons. I could paint; I just didn't know how to demonstrate it, and after a few classes, I was painting up a storm.

We spent twelve intense hours of learning and doing. My brain hurt absorbing so many exciting new thoughts and absorbing the new things we had learned. My mind had been cranking open inch by inch over the past few months. Now it flung open, airing itself out, gulping air fresh with new stimulating knowledge while flushing out some of the old standbys it had stored away. It sprung to life with new ideas and concepts and new areas of possibilities. Renovations began taking place and continue to this day.

CHAPTER FOURTEEN

TERRY'S BIRTHDAY APPROACHED. IT WAS a day of remembering twenty-one other birthdays and all the fun that was mine in making each one special. Oh, how she had loved each and every one! What would have been her twenty-second birthday was not a day of pain or sadness. Somehow, I was comforted from the inside. Some of Terry's close friends sent us cards with their kind thoughts, and a poem I had written for the occasion appeared in the paper that day. The words had come to me out of the blue in a matter of minutes. I knew it was right to have it published in the paper for her friends to commemorate her special day.

Today Terry would have been twenty-two.
In celebration of her life, I ask that her family
and friends think of her today, as we will, with happiness,
thanking God for all the years we have shared with her.

Privately sometime today, say a prayer
for her and recall some
of the happy times you both shared,
and laugh because she loved
you all so much and loved laughter.
And when you dance and are happy,
please think of her then,
for you know while she was dancing,
she was happiest. And when
you love, think of her from time to
time, for she knew love and
was loved. She loved her family,
her friends, her work, and
her life. She cherished you all, and
so I ask that you keep her
in your minds and hearts, for then
the spirit that she is will
truly live forever.

Hoping, since it was her birthday, maybe I would "write" something special from her or receive some kind of a message. I kept trying throughout the day. Nothing was happening though. All I would write was "Love, Terry." Maybe the memorial article in the paper was sufficient after all, and the reason I wrote "Love, Terry" would make itself known to me in the months following.

Toward the middle of October, mom called me from Massachusetts with another bit of strange happening. It seemed while mom was getting ready to go to bed, she thought deeply about Terry and wondered if she was still around and whether she could still hear her when she talked to her. Mom got into bed and fell asleep, thinking of Terry and wondering. The next morning upon awakening, mom noticed that her gold loop pierced earring was missing from her left ear before even getting out of bed. Dad had given them to her a few years before, and she wore them all the time. It was the first time one had come off, and she was frantic. First, mom ran her hands under the pillow behind her and through the sheets. Then, figuring it was under the bed, she put her feet down on the floor to discover the earring sitting neatly inside her slipper. In itself, this was no big deal. It could have fallen there the night before, and mentally she may well have thought that. It was a relief to put the earring back, but she still wondered about it. Was this another of Terry's little acts or just a case of an earring falling out of her ear? Answering her question, the following day, when in her same slipper, the same earring appeared, waiting for her. Coincidence? Not if you knew Terry. Mom just got a big kick out of it and thanked Terry for showing her that she was still around.

Other recollections came in little spurts. Things forgotten pop back into the movie—playing life's story in my mind. Shortly after Terry had died, Jon, Terry's previous boyfriend, came over for a visit. It was then he told me about the incident with the pelicans. As we sat in the Florida room laughing about it, the phone rang. Excusing myself, I went into the kitchen to answer it, but after one ring, it ceased, so I returned to Jon and our conversation. Jon was already laughing. "What's so funny?" I asked. "Terry and I had a signal we used with the telephone. When we wanted to talk with each other and get together, we would always dial and let the phone ring once. If the other person were busy, they would get back when they could, but we always knew when the other person wanted to be with the other." It was not an isolated incident. It happened in the weeks to come, with other visits. Coincidence? How many things did I overlook? How many things may have taken place outside this house with friends? No one will ever know, but by putting these occurrences on paper, seeing them come alive in words, there is a resurgence of another understanding of the nature of God.

October closed her doors with one of Terry's closest friends, celebrating her birthday and remembering her last one spent with Terry. Terry went to her friend's house with birthday gifts the previous year, but specific procedures had to follow before her friend could open them, all Terry's penchant for fun. First, there was a package of balloons they had to blow up, every single one of them. The first part was sitting on the floor of her bedroom amidst the gaily-colored balloons. It took them both quite a while just to blow them all up. The next bit of fun came out of Terry's purse. She had purchased two sets of false noses attached to eyeglasses, and they both had to put them on and sing Happy Birthday. Then she could open her gifts! How well I can picture them both. I can even hear their laughter bouncing off the walls in the house. Those two had many, many fun times together. They could have written their own book, as most young people could.

Sometimes, in particular, were more special or as memorable as Christmas with Terry. Putting some order on the more meaningful holidays would be Christmas in front, followed directly by Halloween and birthdays, hers and her friends. From the very beginning, Terry loved Halloween and dressing up in costumes. We had so much fun getting different outfits together, deciding what she would "go as," digging up material, and finalizing those creations with terrific results. The older Terry became, the more fun and thought went into the costumes. Halloween became even more enjoyable during the last several years when she and her date would get dressed and go out to their favorite nightclub with all their other friends attired in their outfits too. It was about four years ago when Terry put a costume together with my help. She looked more like Wonder Woman than Wonder Woman. Her boyfriend went as Superman, and they ended up winning best costumes. Somehow, I felt there should be some little happening on this particular day, so I had my hopes up on Halloween. Nothing happened as the candy waited by the door for the little trick-or-treaters. Very few children were allowed, at that time, to be a part of this childhood fantasy, and I felt sadness with its apparent ending. There were no young families in our area this year, so we had even fewer than before. Only four very young children, with parents waiting a few feet away, came to our door. Of the four that came, it may have just been another coincidence, but a little blonde-haired, blue-eyed girl dressed as Wonder Woman in a homemade costume came, followed by a little boy dressed as Superman. How glad I was that they came!

Wonder Woman

November showed traces that Christmas was on its way—A Christmas I did not want to face. It just didn't seem fair. How could Christmas come without her? What would I do? What about our secret lists we'd write out and exchange, the mysterious packages hiding under beds and stuffed into closets? Oh, how I wanted to fall asleep and wake up after the New Year had begun. If there were a way to do it safely, I would have canceled living for that period of time and resumed after it was over.

The thought of buying a tree alone seemed a sacrilege. But that had been Terry's and my job, a job painstakingly done for our tree had to be perfect, yet had to have character. The character was what made the tree perfect if that makes any sense at all. It did to us. We would get the tree home and stand it in the living room while it would wait for Don to put the lights on. From there on, the decorating was ours exclusively. At first, Terry dove right into the spirit of things but soon became bored. Inevitably, the rest of the job was mine alone. For the past few years, she had collected all her own decorations and loved each one. Almost all of the decorations belonged to her by now. She cautioned me that soon she would be getting married, and all the decorations would go with her. She said my tree was going to look awful funny, nude.

This year there was no way I could even look at those decorations, let alone think of a tree. Her little treasures remained packed away with all the other decorations. Some things are readily faced, but some things we wisely avoid. Christmas was heading the list on avoidance though I knew I was just kidding myself. I would buy gifts, I would send cards, and I would meet the outside appearances. It was more the thought of it all that I dreaded. It was still November, and I was jumping the gun on being miserable. Picture Christmas morning, especially a few weeks before, remembering when the tree would be up, and Terry would notice whenever a new gift appeared. She had to shake it, squeeze it, and feel it until it almost shouted to her what it was. Her father did the same thing. I just watched the two of them, enjoying this more than when the mystery was over on Christmas morning.

Around the third week in November, Terry sprinkled joy all over my mother's living room. Mom was in the kitchen washing dishes and "talking" to Terry again, telling her once more how much she missed and loved her. Then from the living room came the delightful sound of Mom's music box sitting on the coffee table, playing "Lara's Theme." Mom flew into the room and could almost see Terry standing there, giggling, as the music box flung its tune all around the room, coating everything in its scope with happiness. Finally, mom just stood there between the kitchen and the living room, glued to the spot, staring at the now silent music box. She thanked Terry for dropping in and thanked God for letting these things be, and then went back to the mundane job of washing her dishes. It tickled me when she called. It seemed Terry was either with Mom or me, and I grew curious about where she was in between.

Thanksgiving saw Dan flying home and away from other Thanksgivings spent with us. It was a good choice. Participating in some holidays is a farce when you are grieving, especially family-oriented ones. Who is kidding who? The three of us sitting around our table would have been pitiful with Terry's chair empty. We all canceled. Don and I ate a steak dinner directly in front of the television. The dinner was fine, and Thanksgiving never materialized, nor was it missed. Dan and Terry would fix dinner in years past while Don and I were on the golf course. They would quibble over how to fix all the different vegetables and be triumphant when everything turned out great. I did the cleaning up, but that was a pleasure. Other Thanksgivings and Christmases would come. The first ones were not as bad as we expected, although entering my first store, hearing my first Christmas carol, whisked me right out the door again in tears. No wonder during Christmas, more people commit suicide than at any other time of the year. Aside from it being the date we celebrate the birth of Christ, it is also a day of all our memories bunched together.

Our Christmas was saved by a surprise visit from my sister and brother-in-law, who, knowing how we dreaded this holiday, left their own family to spend it with us. It was the most wonderful, loving gift they could have given. There was a small Areca palm tree in the Florida room. I placed two strings of tiny lights around it, and it was just the right touch. Here was our tree! Presents were placed around it, and Christmas never knew the difference. It was a happy atmosphere and one of the most memorable Christmases we've had.

Dan had gone home for the Christmas holiday as he had in earlier years. He came back to Florida for New Year's Eve, avoiding in every way anything reminding him of the joy of the year before. Terry had flown to Connecticut to be with him for New Year's Eve weekend that year. She had scrimped and saved every cent she could for the trip. Dan's mother drove Terry to the airport for her trip home and told me, long after, that she knew she would never see Terry alive again. It was an overpowering sensation as she held and hugged her before they said goodbye.

Strangely, from this day on until Terry's death, Dan's mother's health failed. I remember Dan voicing his concern about his mother from time to time and talking about all the tests she had been undergoing to determine the problem.

She had lost twenty pounds, was listless, and felt poorly. All the tests came back negative. There was nothing physically wrong with her, and she was baffled. All her symptoms disappeared after Terry died. Apparently, on a level she was unaware of, Terry's death was forecasting itself.

Dan had planned to fly into Melbourne, Florida some time on the thirty-first and call me when he knew the exact time of the flight. He never called the day before, and I went about my everyday business, as I had shopping to do. The store I was heading for was on the way to the airport. Glancing at the airport sign, I decided on a whim to swing down the road to the airport. I could at least pick up a timetable of arriving flights while I was there, so I took a ticket and parked in short-term parking. I dashed into the terminal. With the schedule in my hand, I dodged people while trying to determine when the next flight would arrive, but I couldn't read the darn thing without my glasses, and I had left them home. I stuffed the schedule in my pocketbook while my eyes swept over the swarm of people just disembarking from a flight. A familiar blond head topped the crowd, standing by the baggage pickup.

Dan was standing alone, waiting for his suitcases. It suddenly struck me that maybe he had made previous arrangements to be picked up by someone else, like a girl, and I would embarrass him if he saw me, so I waited for a few minutes watching those around him. Then, satisfied that he was alone, I jostled next to him and said, "Hey, good looking, want a ride?" "What are you doing here?" he asked. "I called you from Atlanta, but no one answered," I told him I wasn't sure myself what I was doing there and that I didn't know when I pulled in. But I sure did now. When we got to the car in the parking lot and checked out with the little ticket, the time I arrived was exactly the minute his plane touched down; another coincidence. My life incorporated a string of them then.

Thinking back, when I did all my funny "writing," I had at one time decided to ask "yes" and "no" questions of whomever I was in contact with. (It was my guides or my higher consciousness, and we all have them, I later learned.) So, I made a "yes" on the upper right-hand side of the paper, "no" on the left, and let my hand with a pen in it guide me where it may. Of course, I always had some religious symbol on the paper for my own peace of mind, whether it was a drawn cross or one of my old medals I wore as a child.

My grandmother gave me one such medal many years ago, and I loved it for its beauty and uniqueness. It was a sterling silver rose-faced metal that had two pieces to it. The top medal and bottom medal swung clear of each other, the top half fitting over the bottom, giving the appearance of one single medal. On the insides and back of each piece were engraved religious figures in minute detail. Unfortunately, my silver chain had broken, and though I never bothered to have it repaired, I always carried the medal with me. Then, one day, while showing Rose how I placed the medal on the paper, she picked up my medal, looked at it, and told me her grandmother had one just like it.

An added meaning for my grandmother to have that particular medal dawned on me. I don't know why I never put two and two together. My grandmother's name was Rose. I looked at this other coincidence and saw something but was not able to label it. It was at this time I felt a need for Rose to know Terry through photographs, ones that showed the real Terry, unlike those seen in the newspapers.

When I handed Rose Terry's pictures, she looked through them all, then held one and stared at it. I was very aware she was staring, not just looking, for it certainly would have been appropriate for her to say how lovely she was and just hand me back the pictures, but she just stared. It would not be until February of the upcoming year that I would know why Rose did so. In February, it would be my time to stare. New Year's Eve looked the other way, and Don and I slipped past it, another grateful step. We watched television and went to bed early. This year, said the calendar, was over.

CHAPTER FIFTEEN

Every other weekend, Lorraine would spend the night. These were memorable times when we could always talk about everything that had happened after Terry's death and how it had changed our lives, our way of thinking, and our very concept of life. Her daughters had all "talked" with Terry after her death, and Lorraine was grateful they had had this experience, especially Heather. Heather became closer to Terry after death than before. Lorraine and I were reading everything we could get our hands on, trying to understand more about things we had never before questioned. There was so much humor in our search then, and there still is. Our intensity sometimes gave way to gales of laughter and tears. No one ever said learning had to be a painful experience.

During her weekly treks, an elderly man Lorraine had met at the laundromat supplied her with metaphysical books to read. We took turns devouring them first and then discussing them afterward, which inevitably led us into deep conversations and questions we finally found answers to.

The following January, the idea of writing this story materialized. Every event, big and small, and a little voice inside me saying, "I should write a book." Finally, I took the little voice seriously, but since I knew little about writing a book, I called Rose.

"Fran, that's a great idea!" she urged, and since I knew nothing about writing or how to start, Rose suggested I read a book written years ago by another mother who had lost her daughter. The book was called 'Always, Karen,' a true story of a young woman, an only child, who had died in her early twenties of cancer. After her death, Karen communicated with her mother too, but in a somewhat different manner. The book sounded interesting. I needed something like this to see how I would handle it, how much was said, and if our stories paralleled each other. So, after talking with Rose, within five minutes, I was at the library searching.

The book I was looking for was out of print. I checked different libraries, hoping to find a copy. No luck. I wanted that book and was bound to get it. Yet I knew if something is meant to be yours and you do all in your power to get it and it still is not yours, maybe you simply were not meant to have it. Begrudgingly, I admitted this might be the case but still did not want to believe it. The same evening, I called Lorraine. I was feeling depressed and really down. Pursuing the book wasn't mentioned at the time. I just wanted to talk. She reminded me she would be over the following night, and thoughts of that cheered me up. After hanging up, I felt better. Finally, there was something to look forward to.

The next evening as Lorraine and I relaxed together,

relating the past week's events and catching up on what was new with each of us, she mentioned that the older man from the laundromat had given her another stack of books to read. Of course, that was always good news, and this time it brought more than news. Lorraine, sensing my depression of the night before, felt that in the stack of books that the man had given her was one that could especially help me somehow. So, she dumped them all out on her bed at home and randomly selected one to bring to me.

As she was telling me this, I looked at her and said, my heart beating crazily, "I know the name of the book! It's 'Always Karen', isn't it?'"

"How on earth did you know that?" she asked me. "I just knew" was all I could say. I was obviously meant to have that book!

"Always, Karen," had many similarities in the experiences of Karen's mother and myself, as there were in the two girls. After reading it, it helped me formulate my own story and gave me a rough idea of how to begin. With Karen's mother, the writing of her story was automatic. She just sat down, and it "came," writing and all.

I thought that just maybe if I sat down at the typewriter, the whole story would gush out, and I wouldn't have to do a thing. Picturing me now, sitting there at the keys, waiting for the story to blurt out, makes me laugh. It didn't work that way at all, but I had to give it a shot. There were many such instances of automatic typing I had read about, so I had nothing to lose, and I lost.

The same thing applied to automatic writing. Hopefully, I would sit with pen in hand, waiting for some profound things to come forth. Most of the time, nothing but graceful swirls and designs floated across the paper, but sometimes there were exceptions. This time, I sat down with my pen and paper and blanked out my mind. I asked Terry if I should write a story about all this, and stashed away somewhere, still in my jumble of notes, was the answer given me,

"Yes, write the story. You will have help, wonderful help."

For this reason, I thought I would just sit down at the typewriter or pick up a pen and zap; the story would appear. That's what "wonderful help" meant to me. Half the time, I was unaware of who I was talking to when I did this writing. Now I realize besides Terry, I was talking to my own higher consciousness, something I had never even heard about.

All I knew was that I was "me," now I was finding out who "me" really was, a definite awareness of the presence of God within myself. To those who have experienced something similar, this is the awakening within you, one that cannot be put aside or dismissed. Someone knocked on the door to "me," and I faced a stranger when I opened the door. But the stranger that came in was me! So, the meeting between me and myself goes on, as does the growing awareness of everything on earth and beyond. What a world! What a God!

It looked like in my writing this story; it would be just the typewriter and me, no special effects. So, I gathered all my pages of writings and scribbles, covering pages and pages, pieced together my notes of all the little things that happened, put them in some semblance of order, and began to write. Luckily, I wrote most of them down as they happened and dated them. Had I not, I might forget some, and there were more incidences I believe that did happen, that at the time, I wasn't open to. What a shame I missed some. How many people, though, who are grieving, today ignore them all? From time to time, my thoughts always wandered to the families of the other women who Wilder murdered. Was there a chance this was happening to any of them? How would I know? Even if I knew how to get in touch with them, I don't know how to ask them.

I began to have thoughts, my own thoughts, to the understanding that Jesus meant to be the Way-shower of what we could be. He could heal the sick, could appear and disappear, and Jesus could die but yet not die. He came as an example of God's love for us, as God's example of perfection in man, every man. Why would God create this man with these abilities if it were not to show us that we had the same abilities because we, too, were manifestations of His love?

Jesus was the standard of excellence that we could achieve if we so desired. Christ himself studied as He taught, but He left himself open as a pure channel to the Holy Spirit. It is how Jesus worked his miracles. Did God ever say He gave us less? Are our minds closed? What are we afraid of?

Are we afraid of the truth that sets us free? Think of all the things that never would have been if there had not been someone who said, "Why not?" Can't you almost hear God saying, "Boy, I give them an example of what they can be and what do they do? They worship the example and miss the whole point, the miracle they each are!"

It seems we had taken God and His truths, and for our own selfish beliefs, reworked His words to fit our needs. God is love. How we have devastated the world with our rules and regulations, with what is right and what is wrong. How He must wince when He watches and listens to us. What we do in His name is a crime.

My imagination ran full steam ahead, guessing and thinking of all possibilities to the questions in my life. Somehow it only seemed natural that a seminar, "The Awakened Imagination," would find both Lorraine and me absorbing whatever new knowledge we could. It was to be another beginning in inner growth for us both. An internationally known master, author, and musician conducted the seminar. The main gist of the workshop was awareness.

The word "awareness" looks like such an innocent little word, but it packs the biggest punch in the dictionary. Awareness is the beginning of everything in life. Without it, man becomes nothing more than a struggling prisoner in his own restricted cell of life, with no outlook but bleakness. With awareness comes sunrises, blinding with electrifying light in colors never dreamed about, shouting of the joy of life and ending the slumber of sleeping souls, shaking them awake to witness the dawning of themselves.

Of imagination, Albert Einstein stated, "Imagination is more important than knowledge. Knowledge is limited. Imagination encircles the world." The seminar lasted all day, with a break late in the afternoon for dinner. It was at dinner when I learned why Rose had stared at Terry's picture months before.

Rose had invited us to join her and her friends at a particular restaurant and Lorraine, and I accepted. It was at the restaurant that coincidences piled almost too high for me, and the biggest one slammed into me like a speeding truck. Rose introduced me to her daughter, and my eyes swam. She could have been Terry's sister. The resemblance was so striking. It wasn't just the outside appearance, but I saw what she was like inside, and it, too, was Terry.

For the first time in a long time, my heart hurt again. Lorraine, sitting next to me, was staring too. First, she stared at Rose's daughter, then at me, wondering how long I could sit calmly with someone who looked so much like my daughter. For a split second, I admit, I was ready for flight, but it passed, and I remained seated, watching Rose and her daughter chat and have fun as Terry and I used to do so many times. Terry had a crazy grin she reserved for family only. It was one in which she would screw up her face and look smugly stupid if such a thing were possible. During their conversation, Rose's daughter flashed that same grin. I didn't know what to think, except I knew it hurt. Enough is enough. If this were some sort of a test for me, then I would pass it and not make a fool of myself. I tried not to stare too much. That was all I could do. I had never encountered someone who had so many of Terry's physical and inner characteristics before. This was why Rose had so much emotion on her face when she stared at my pictures of Terry that day in her office months ago. She knew, and she shared with me later that she was staring at her own daughter too and that Terry took the place of her daughter. Our daughter's changed life's tracks.

The choice was theirs. Terry took the track that led her to Christopher Wilder and death. Rose explained that when we are born, we all enter life with many different paths to choose from, and we can change these same tracks by the many choices we make. Our future is not set in stone. Anything and everything we desire has already been created and exists for us on one of our life tracks. What determines your future are your thoughts, beliefs about what you think is possible, and commitment to the desired result. Sometimes I felt like I was on a movie set of "The Twilight Zone."

It was February. My parents were visiting when Chele', my niece, came to visit too. Our house was full, and no matter how I tried, tension began to mount, an underlying thing that watched and built itself slowly. It was a feeling of uneasiness and unrest, even while all was quiet to the naked eye. Something unpleasant was building and was taking its time, nurturing its infection of our senses. There had been a growing awareness of the dissolving relationship between Don and me. He was always involved in his work, and I, with all that was happening surrounding Terry's death. We went in opposite directions, pretending not to notice, even though my sister had reminded me of the undeniably high percentages of divorces among those who had lost a child as we had. Instead of growing together, somewhere along the way, we drifted further and further apart. The game of living together became just that. As March approached, we began a replay of the year before, this time without Terry; no one was saying anything of the approaching date of her death, but all were helplessly watching as the day came into view. It is worse trying to forget than it is to remember. We were all different, trying to act the same somehow.

This past year, though, I had learned the benefits of meditation and did so for fifteen minutes every day. Each morning after Don went to work, I would tell Mom and Dad not to disturb me, and I would close the door to my room and quietly open the door to myself. This was my listening time, the part of the day put aside exclusively for God and me alone. The everyday garbage of living was set aside and not allowed to enter. My mind, working in reverse of the artist struggling to get down something on his canvas, I tried keeping the canvas of my mind blank. With a clear mind, only then could I listen to the true artist, our Creator.

One morning while I sat in silence in my bedroom, my thoughts drifted to Terry and where she was in the universe of our existence. I released the thought, finished meditating, and returned to the living room to find Mom staring wide-eyed at me. "What's the matter?" She answered, "While you were in your room a few minutes ago, I was daydreaming out this window, thinking of Terry, when a voice startled me, saying, "Here, now." I looked around to see who was talking, and no one was there!" It was a soft, barely discernable whisper, but a voice, nevertheless. Could the power of our combined thoughts have reached her somehow, somewhere, and she, for a brief second, communicated back? Extraordinary things happening to ordinary people, why? How frustrating it was not to have the answers, but how fascinating it was to search for them, and maybe they are not extraordinary things but ordinary after all.

March 18th appeared and disappeared. I was happy my niece was there, particularly on that day. It was fun to have her around. She lifted my spirits without saying a word. A few cards of remembrance arrived, and the day passed relatively painlessly for me. I was surprised. A Memorial Mass that we all attended was said for Terry, but we didn't allow the occasion to darken our day too much. There had been enough suffering, and I felt no need to isolate and dwell on the day she decided to leave this earth.

Our minds ticked off the moments of this day, though, re-enacting the previous year's events, one by one, knowing where she was almost hour by hour at this same time. The rest of the family called on the telephone. Friends called too, just to say they knew what day it was and that we were in their thoughts. Kindness helps so much in renewing happier thoughts. I hoped that Terry would mark this day with some small proof of her continued existence, but the day passed dully without anything unusual taking place. It seems when we expect something and wait anxiously, it never materializes. But if you are not thinking or expecting anything, a surprise is undoubtedly waiting for you, and there was one waiting for me!

Mom and Dad had gone back to Massachusetts. Chele' remained another two weeks to soak up some more sun before going back herself. We enjoyed each other's company, shopping, talking, and getting to know one another as persons other than as "aunt "or "niece." I had always loved Chele' because she was my sister's daughter. Now I loved her for her.

One morning, Chele' was still sleeping as I prepared to leave the house. I remember it was a little before 9:00 AM when I suddenly realized I had to put Terry out of my mind more and move ahead with my life. A part of my life had ended. I had to put things in proper perspective. It hurt thinking this way, but I knew I must go on with my thoughts of the future and put my mind on Don and me, where it belonged.

Torrents of tears came with this new pain, moving out of the past and into the future without Terry. I reached for a tissue on the kitchen table, feeling only empty pain inside me. The box was empty. I walked into the bathroom and WHOOSH! It felt as though someone had thrown Johnson's Love's Baby Soft Powder directly into my face and nose, the powder she always used. The smell was so sweet and overpowering, I choked on it! It now whirled in my nostrils and dried my tears with its scent.

Elation, joy, and gratitude replaced the painful sensations of just moments before! Terry was saying everything was okay, and she would always be checking in with me. There would be no end to her, for love does not end. But, in order to grow, sometimes you must let go. Letting go is the hard part, and as I released my hold on the part of Terry that I had to deal with, I was rewarded for doing so. This joy I felt, knowing her presence, can't be verbalized. There are no words to express all that was inside me. Instead, I wanted to shout it and share it! The glory of positively knowing that there is no such thing as death! None!

Feeling elated again, I headed for my car to run some errands. I had only driven a few hundred yards down the street when I felt the urge to turn on the radio and listen. Switching it on, the only words I heard were a song sung by Stevie Wonder, "I just called to say I love you, I just called to say how much I care, I just called to say I love you and I mean it from the bottom of my heart." I drove back to the house because I was splashing tears of joy all over myself, and I wanted to get myself back together while relishing it all.

Chele' was awake, sitting at the kitchen table when I walked in, and was delighted to hear of Terry's unexpected visit. The only thing now that was puzzling me was why this particular day? Why not on March 18th? Checking the calendar, I saw it was the twenty-seventh. The date meant nothing to me before, but it sure did now, and I had to figure out if there was any significance to Terry's dropping in. It didn't take me long.

The book given us by the funeral director, recording all the details of the wake and funeral was in Terry's room, sitting on her desk. March 27th was the day Terry was buried. The funeral mass began at 9:00 A.M. Today was one year to the day. I won't forget the date now, not because of the funeral and sadness, but of all the joy she brought me one year later. And whenever I see Johnson's Baby Powder on the grocery shelves, I smile and don't even wonder anymore where the powder smell came from that day. I had thrown out her powder months before. What difference did it make after all? On the first anniversary of her burial, Terry had remembered, and I had not.

My niece left the first part of April. Don and I were finally alone, and we watched the days slide by while trying to get our lives back on an even keel. All the dreaded days had passed without Terry's physical presence. All the "firsts," the first Halloween, the first Christmas, her birthday, even the anniversary of her death had been met, only to find that the dreading was worse than the event itself. Doors were gently closing behind each special day, but there was still one more part of Terry's life left on the threshold. Just as I felt I had finally experienced all the emotions surrounding her death, a new one entered.

This one had been so far into the future when Terry had been killed; I never gave it much thought. But now it was happening. Dan was graduating from the Florida Institute of Technology in Melbourne and was preparing to go home to Connecticut. We had bought him a handsome gold bracelet as our graduation present to match the chain he wore around his neck. I believe I had a little help from Terry in the selection. Dan's parents flew down for the ceremony, and we all got together the night before for dinner at a nearby restaurant.

The food was excellent. It was a dining pleasure that blended with pleasant conversation. Only once did I glimpse a sad expression on Dan's face while he talked of going home. It shadowed his eyes for only moments, and no one seemed to notice but me. The evening went on and left us behind, making small talk, filling time with our words, saying nothing of consequence. After graduation, Dan's parents flew back. Dan would drive home a few days later, packing into his car what his parents couldn't take with them.

He came over late that afternoon to say goodbye. The last door was now ajar. While he sat and talked with my husband, my inner voice was saying, "Oh, Please Dan, just get up, don't say a word, don't look into my eyes, just go." But their conversation continued. They both stood up, and my husband walked out to Dan's car alone, giving me a chance to say my own goodbyes. Instead, I broke down in his arms and somewhat pushed him out the door, telling him if I snapped out of my sorry state, I'd come out and wave him off, which I ended up doing.

This day, this goodbye, this moment in time, had hung in the future like a bad picture. It was almost over. With Dan leaving, half of Terry's heart was making its exit now, a part of Terry that was never mine, heading for the future and leaving us as was necessary, in the past. With all of my being, I silently wished him the best. He was taking more than himself with him, oh, so very much. Part of Terry left this house with him, and that part of her will remain with him forever. On his heart is carved her initials, hidden from view but embedded within him, and he knows this. Dan and I have touched souls. He may leave this house and this area, but a part of him too, will I carry in my heart, now scored with his initials. As his car disappeared from view, I saw not one but two figures inside.

On July 11th, wondering how to end this part of my story, I walked into Terry's room. While standing by her bed, her door gently swung closed behind me. There were no open windows, no breezes. Completing this part of the story gave me an overwhelming sense that this was merely the tip of the iceberg of spiritual knowledge and growth, and as you read on, you will see, I was so right! Behind the next door was the treasure of knowledge Terry's death led me. A pact we had made before birth.

This pact was no random thing, no vow made lightly, as many are in today's world. It was a sacred trust, a promise written in stone we both made before we were born. It was well-planned and thought out, in many instances, tried on as we do new clothing before the final purchase to see if it was the perfect fit for our own personal needs. Life is a precious gift and not taken lightly by us before we are born. What are our needs, we ask? And in asking, the answers come. Our lives are only about spiritual growth, lessons to learn, knowledge to garner. To finally know who we truly are is life's purpose.

We know of what we yearn to have knowledge and experience. We have many choices, and it is we who make our final choice. Before birth, we are fully aware of what our life will hold for us, and like those new clothes we may buy, we are aware of how they will fit because our life is known to us before our first breath. Our soul aches for the gift this upcoming life will hold, be it joy, happiness, pain, or sorrow, for us and those we love. Gifts received, gifts given, over and over again.

The newborn baby we hold in our arms is not new at all, but a very old soul, realizing its own dream through its birth. In birth, our soul begins to fulfill the plan laid out long before our entrance into the world in the physical body. In birth we begin our chosen life and in death we fulfill our own prophecy.

Part Two

CHAPTER SIXTEEN

A NEW DOOR I NEVER IMAGINED opening now stared me in the face.

After Terry's death, I wasn't aware of the danger of our marriage dissolving. But I later came to understand we all change and grow, sometimes in different directions and not consciously aware of it. Part of me loved him, and the other part felt disconnected. Have you ever looked back at a specific time in your life and wondered how you got through it or how you did what you did at the time? Leaving my husband was one of those things or times that now, when I look back, I wonder how the heck I did it, and, at the same time, I know. Something had changed within me, and I was unaware of it. I had changed, or maybe I just became my real self, not a perceived notion of who I thought I was. I had begun to meet my real self for the very first time. This new self, the real me, one that lies dormant under the guise of who I thought I should be, emerged. It was amazing to be consciously in the body of this new woman!

I loved my husband, and I had no intention in the world of leaving him. There was no plan in my mind or heart to do so, but I did. One day the words came out of my mouth and stunned him. It stunned me too. There was no anger on my part at all. It was just time to leave, and I did, and all the time, it was as if I were in a dream. It was something you would see in a movie, but for me, this was for real. For me, our marriage had reached the stage of completion.

Remembering years ago, I had a favorite priest, Father Quinn. This same priest, years later, was to say the funeral mass for my daughter. Father Quinn was a theologian, different from the other priests, and it set him apart. People always crowded into every Mass he presided over because of his profound spiritual wisdom, sense of humor, and wit.

At one sermon, he said he firmly believed that if the good Lord knew how long our life expectancy would eventually be, He never would have made marriage a life-long commitment. Everyone in the church chuckled, but maybe it's true. Could it be that after we experience all we need to experience from being in a relationship with someone, gain all there is to gain, it's okay to move on? When you squeeze a relationship dry, do you hang on to what's left? Have you fulfilled all your promises? Are all marriages meant to last a lifetime? Now, I don't think so. Some are, some are not. But, of course, there's where the wisdom to know the difference comes into play. When the time is right, we give ourselves the courage to step outside the bubble of our so-called reality and into who we really are: like stepping out of our own body and into another who looks just like us, but has the wisdom the other does not.

Since Terry's death, I have been continuously drawn

to learning what happens when we die, and with Terry's antics after her death, I just needed to know things. There were answers I needed to questions still unanswered. My questions began with "why?" That's where my story leads you, to the answers and how you can find them. If Terry had not been killed, chances are, some of this knowledge would not have been yours or mine.

The need to know more, to understand precisely where God, the God of my childhood, fits into Terry's death; that's partially what drove me. That's why I had to leave everything that was safe and familiar. There was an aloneness inside me that I could fill only with knowledge, and I wasn't even sure what kind of knowledge I was searching for. The information Rose had given me spurred me on to want more and search for more. Leaving my husband had nothing to do with him at all; it was a longing deep inside me that proved stronger than our marriage vows.

The many classes I had taken with Rose lit a fire of inquiry, constantly fed with new material. This fire burned brightly all the time. After Terry's death, I had read so many books, each bringing whole, fresh ways to look at life and at death itself. I was fascinated by what it was alluding to-our own Divine plan. Today, embedded within my consciousness and not so deep I can't tap into the knowledge, is all I learned from taking classes with Rose. These classes eventually drew me away from Florida to Georgia within years of Terry's death. My family and friends faded into the background as new knowledge gave birth to another brand-new existence for me. Terry's death had propelled me with an undeniable force away from everything safe and comfortable, and known into the unknown. You see, after Terry was killed and I understood she truly did continue to exist as we all do, my whole being wanted to know more. Perhaps this is part of what drove me to continue to live and hope. The religion that had, in the past, brought answers no longer supplied them to those questions my heart sought. I had lots of questions, lots of questions. Though belief in God remained a mainstay, and God, my foundation of beliefs, I felt something was missing and had no idea what that might be. It was like knowing God on the surface but also knowing there was something deeper, much more profound, a deeper knowledge I had not even tapped. And I wanted to. This is why I found it easy that day to drive out of my comfortable, safe life and home I shared with my husband; without a doubt, that is what I was supposed to do, crazy as it seemed to family and friends.

I was learning that the devastation felt by my daughter's death was leading me on a journey to either hope or despair, and it was up to me and no one else, how my life would end up. Now I knew heartbreak could lead to a new beginning in life and not necessarily to a tragic end.

Many times I would wonder why I kept living after Terry was killed. What kept me going? What keeps us all going? The questions tormented me at times until the answer came. The answer came out of my mouth in a clear voice I didn't recognize, and it startled me: "hope," a beautiful word.

Though lying dormant within all of us, hope is triggered in countless ways-a bird singing its little heart out, a sunrise that takes our breath away, the giggle of a little child. We were born with it, and without the possibility of hope, all is indeed lost. Without hope, we lose life's luster forever, and trust ceases to exist.

This gift of hope is what we all cling to at one time or another. Our safe harbor in the storm is the light that shows us the way and is God's lasting gift. Hope is all that kept me living after I lost Terry, and at the same time, what on earth was I hoping for? That was not about to change with my only child dead, I still experienced pain and sorrow, which seemed inescapable. But this strong, pulsating light of hope held me warmly in its arms, just like the mother of a small frightened child, and said to me, "There, there, everything is going to be all right, "and hope was right.

CHAPTER SEVENTEEN

HOPE LED ME TO THE Swan Center Monastery, where, after taking countless classes from Rose, I began experiencing a new way of life and living. Leaving my organized religion behind me, I embraced a spiritual path known as Swanéte. This is an ancient spiritual philosophy based on a core belief that we are all here to love and serve God by loving and serving all of God's creations and finding our own life's purpose while doing so. It was here I became a spiritual student, and my training began.

After a twelve-year apprenticeship under the headmaster of the Swanéte monastery in Tibet, Rose was initiated as a Swanéte Master in 1986. To many of you who are not familiar with this title, maybe I can shed a little light on the subject. If you look up "master" or God-realized master," you will find tons of information. A God-realized master is a commanding and impressive person, and this person is one you only seek when all else but the spiritual path matters to you. Perhaps this is where the saying, "When the student is ready, the master appears," came into being. Masters have taught timeless spiritual truths in various methods, and their teachings reflect the environment and period in which they live. A master practices what they preach and live it 24 hours a day. As students, we had the honor of observing these qualities every day without wavering. Master Rose's mission is to train others to be spiritual masters.

Master Rose's first task as a Swanéte Master was to establish the Swanéte philosophy as a spiritual organization in the United States. In 1987, Master Rose opened The Swan Center for Intuitive Living- a Swanéte public learning center in Atlanta, Georgia. The Center housed a seminar company, holistic healing clinic, a fine arts gallery and music hall, offices for life coaching, and the Swanéte Mystery School. The Swan Center for Intuitive Living is currently based in California, where Master Rose serves as headmaster.

In October 1989, Master Rose established the Swan Center Monastery in Marble Hill, Georgia, to train Swanéte priests and masters. The Swan Center Monastery housed a welcome center, seminar rooms, a spiritual retreat center, gardens, nature trails for meditation, and horseback riding, a petting zoo, and a stable and arena for horse training, dog partnership clinics, children's camps, and riding clinics. The monastery also served as an animal rescue and educational Center, which led to the formation of Swan Center Outreach, a 501©(3) non-profit organization.

Master Rose combined her two loves in life; helping animals and people. She incorporated the rescue and rehabilitation of abused and neglected animals into the spiritual training matrix for her students, giving them greater personal awareness and a clearer understanding of how to love and serve God and humanity at the highest level.

If you could imagine meeting God in disguise, relinquishing our childhood picture of what we thought God looked like, usually an older man with a long beard, here is what you would see. On the outside, in the physical, she looked like any other woman, but after that, all similarities were gone. If you were fortunate to meet her, right away you knew. A master radiates love and peace. You would have to be dead not to sense it. Though not able to put your finger on it, you would know something was different in how you felt in her presence. She can be the spark that ignites the flame of change in your life. If you had fears, they melted away; if you had heartache, they too were lifted, and when you gazed into her eyes, you saw wisdom, light, love, and humor. Yes, humor, because God certainly has the most incredible sense of humor of all. My years at the monastery were filled with her laughter ringing over the paddock or in the barn. I think laughter is one of God's greatest gifts. Laughter lifts the soul and carries it with wings up and out of any perceived bit of misery to get a better view of any situation, so you can see it for what it is and change it.

Sometimes in a flood of emotion, my appreciation and love for her leave me almost wordless, and I overflow with the very same love she gives freely to me and everyone. It comes in waves, and for some things and feelings there simply aren't words. When we are touched by pure love, we change. There is no choice. We are the same, yet different, and better, much better. We become a part of that pure love, and it becomes part of us, something we don't ever want to lose but to share with others.

CHAPTER EIGHTEEN

SWAN CENTER MONASTERY WAS SNUGGLED into the foothills of the mountains of North Georgia where I was drawn both literally and physically. Loving animals as I do, I wanted to make this special place happen and help in every way I could. The monastery was something we all helped build with our own two hands. It was a daunting task but taken on with enthusiasm, energy, and lots of love and laughter. We actually chopped down the trees needed to build an enormous barn that would protect and serve all the horses and, eventually, house students. We built a chicken coop that created a safe haven for the chickens, sheep, and goats and constructed corrals and fenced-in areas to keep all animals safe.

It was a beautiful place, where each night, every star in the universe could be seen with such clarity it felt as though you could simply reach up and grab a handful just for yourself. It was the place visitors came to leave behind the problems and stresses they carried. Mother Nature lovingly absorbed and dispensed with them. People would walk the nature trails or go on horseback rides through the forest, and all would comment on the peace they felt when they first stepped onto the property. Peace was everywhere, warmly tangled up like a piece of angora yarn with the many animals covering the grounds, safely in paddocks, barns, and fenced-in areas, eager to greet the arriving guests.

I remember underprivileged children arriving by bus from the city; their little faces lit up as they disembarked. The children looked around in wonderment as they inhaled the pine-scented air and experienced the silence of the foothills, broken only by the whinny of one of our horses, a far cry from the sounds and smells of city streets left behind.

There were children's riding camps, ending in a public horse show. The kids exhibited all they learned and the fears they conquered on horseback, proving to themselves their capabilities were more than even they thought possible. I remember the parents in the bleachers, hearts filled with pride, cheering them on with tears of joy at their accomplishments. Every child won a ribbon, an award, for something. There were no losers. All were winners, always finding something to celebrate about themselves.

To most people, "monastery" connotes hooded figures walking serenely about in a prayer-like mode. This was not at all what this monastery was. Our monastery was filled with a tapestry of rescued animals: horses, goats, dogs, cats, sheep, etc., all needing our love and attention and, in return, giving us handful of students, the training we required. Here, I learned that animals have souls too. They weren't just doled out to the human species by God. We are all on this journey together. We are here for each other to teach, learn and grow. The animals in our lives are not here by accident, they all came here with a purpose as we did, and their goal is to teach us. This was the place to be if you loved animals, and I loved animals.

In the early morning hours, entering the barn, you could hear the soft nickering of the horses patiently waiting for you to bring their feed. These were sacred moments when humans and animals, in silence, communicated on a deeper level with each other and found their common ground.

As I look back at certain occurrences at the monastery and see what I was experiencing at that time, I now see it differently. You see, horses were our spiritual training matrix. The students cared for, trained, and rode horses assigned to them every day. On this particular day, I went down to one of the paddocks to groom one of my most loved horses. Shadow, was a pinto pony (brown and white) who was getting up there in years and as stubborn as a mule when it came to having his hooves picked. He would happily allow you to clean three feet but glued that last leg down to the earth with the force of cement. Now I see he reflected my stubbornness, but I didn't realize it then. This time as I sighed in surrender to his wishes, suddenly, Shadow and I blended into one another. Nothing separated us. We were one. It was over in a matter of seconds, leaving me puzzled. I now know, years later, God was showing me we are all one. The only separation that occurs is in our mind. Shadow was chosen to show me there was no separation at all. I was blessed later to have the same experience with another horse but, at that time, did not fully grasp the gift I had been given, a glimpse into the God-consciousness. "We are all one." It was years later that I finally truly understood.

While at the monastery, we had weekly in-depth spiritual classes that had all of us students clamoring and receiving more knowledge. Now, in hindsight, many years later, I can't remember everything. It's like trying to remember what you learned in your first grade in school. You know you learned a lot, and you realize the information learned was the very building blocks that built the foundation of all that you have become today. But you can't recollect each building block in itself. We had daily classes too, and I must say, one of my favorites was dog obedience. Since we rescued animals, we had an abundance of them, primarily dogs and horses, and they all needed training. Master Rose patiently taught us how to train them, and at that point in my life, I had no idea what a perfect relationship with a dog or horse looked like or was supposed to look like. I learned that humans are supposed to be the pack leader or the lead mare in a herd. At the same time, we were shown the correlation between training animals and training our minds: another life- changing piece of knowledge. For all the years to follow, every one of my dogs knew I was the leader. They could look to me for whatever was needed. All of my dogs, since then, went through the same training I received many years ago.

Being our matrix for training, the horses were exciting and definitely challenging as each horse had their very own personality and quirks, just like us humans. Master Rose allowed us the opportunity to see ourselves through the all-knowing eyes of the horse because they sense our energy, respond to it, and mirror back to us the exact way we are being and feeling. This was a jewel of knowledge in itself.

Here at the monastery, spiritual growth happened in many unexpected ways.

From our horses, we learned compassion and trust from caring for them, which included compassion for ourselves for errors in our own past.

We learned the feeling of freedom and power from riding them because, as God's children, we are free and powerful.

From a disciplined schedule, we learned we could do anything we put our trained mind to do and more than ever imagined possible.

From an organic diet, our bodies responded with health it hadn't realized and knowledge that would stay with us the rest of our lives.

Our animal communication classes taught us we are all

one, connected by love itself, and animals, all creatures great and small, have souls and are here on this planet to be our teachers, healers, and friends.

Many of these same horses are still with us after moving from Georgia to California. All these years later, they remain a testimony to all the loving and compassionate care they continue to receive and have received over the years.

It's obvious the Swan Center Monastery was where the major part of my change took hold, and it was Master Rose's teachings that catapulted me from a grief-stricken mother to a strong, joyful woman.

Part Three

CHAPTER NINETEEN

SCROLLING BACK THROUGH THE YEARS, back to the point where my daughter was killed, I see them now as stepping stones to where I am today. Although they were small steps in themselves, over a long period of time, they were major steps in knowledge, consciousness, and accomplishment. My desire is to bring you to where I am today and save you the years and tears it took me to get me here. I now know for a certainty that Terry's death, anyone's death, was never what it appeared to be. It really isn't the end of their lives at all. It is their own beginning of a new, better life, and that they were the architect of their own life and death for their own soul's purpose. Any sadness is on our part, not theirs.

After Terry was killed and I understood she indeed did continue to exist, as we all do, my whole being wanted to know more. Perhaps this is part of what drove me to continue to live and to hope. The religion that had, in the past, brought answers no longer supplied them to questions my heart sought answers to. I had lots of questions, lots of questions. Though belief in God remained a mainstay, and God, my foundation of beliefs, I felt something was missing and had no idea what that might be. It was like knowing God on the surface but also knowing there was something deeper, more profound, a knowledge I had not even tapped into the depth of. And I wanted to. The absorption of this knowledge did not happen suddenly. Where an acorn was planted, an oak tree now stands. And the knowledge I gained that everything has already been created for us to draw from and mold through our thoughts, desires, and beliefs did not begin suddenly. It reminds me of gardening, a passion of mine.

When we plant a garden, the soil has to be tilled and weeds removed for the seeds to take hold, grow and flower. The monastery was my mind's garden. This is where the person I am today began. Who I was then and who I am now are two different people. We have the same souls, same body, but a new awareness that changes our world. The seed that was planted in the garden had no idea what had to take place for it to flourish; it was just a seed with a longing to be more, a seed of change. It didn't care about the work that was required for all its needs to be met to begin a new life. And when the seed sprouted, was it aware of the nurturing required to sustain this life? Probably not, but there was a master gardener there who did.

The master gardener had a plan, a divine one, and it was to love and nurture these seeds to full maturity, keeping them happy, loved, and fulfilled. It certainly wasn't an easy task because these seeds were human beings, students, with minds and ideas of their own. Oh, they may have understood they were in this garden for growth, but their minds had trouble grasping it. Struggle was no stranger, but many times, struggle is a precursor to growth.

When I plant my own garden, I already know the potential of what I am growing. I can see what this plant will look like when it matures. And that is what I cultivate, always having in mind the end result of my labor of love. Does the seed itself know its own potential? I don't know, but I know if you just throw seeds onto the ground and just walk away, you won't have a beautiful garden. It takes work, first from you, the gardener, and then from the seed and plant itself, to respond to all you have given it. This was a good description of me when I was at the monastery, in seed form. I had no idea how deep my soul was planted in the desire to blossom, nor did I have an understanding of who I was and why I truly existed. At that time, I thought I had no purpose, especially since I was no longer a mother. With your only child dead, how could I be called that? But there was the master gardener who did know, and it was always her knowledge, wisdom and clear picture that kept me going.

My own garden, I call my mind, was freshly tilled every day at the monastery. The nutrients that went into the soil to enrich it were knowledge, in small doses, and were totally unrecognizable because of the many different tasks performed to achieve this. We all coped with this infusion of knowledge in various ways because we all had different gardens (minds). Some minds conformed like obedient little children, some did not. But looking back and even jumping into the present, I look at all the years that have passed, and these very same people with these same minds, though trained now, still surround me in love and friendship. That is saying a lot. We all went through a training phase at the monastery, not completely knowing what we were learning because it was so gradual. A great example of this was the movie, "The Karate Kid", wax on, wax off. Looking back, it becomes a clear, crisp picture of what we all learned because of the love, wisdom, and devotion of one woman, Master Rose Ashley, our master gardener. She was, and is, the spark that ignites the flame of change you desire in your life.

As days and months stretched into years, the domino effect of Terry's death became crystal clear. It had been a "Wax on, Wax off" affair. I didn't realize how much I was learning or that I was in a preparatory state of learning even more. There's an old Zen saying, "Before enlightenment, chop wood, carry water. After enlightenment, chop wood, carry water." It means no matter how much you know, you still have to take out the garbage. The difference is you take it out with more consciousness. Everything Master Rose Ashley taught me changed who I was. It was done in increments without me even knowing it was happening, beginning at the monastery decades ago. Lifetimes of beliefs faded before my unsuspecting eyes. I was transformed into someone I never knew existed, my real self, from a cocoon to a butterfly, and this butterfly is still learning and morphing into more than I could think possible.

One of the most life-changing pieces of knowledge gained from all my experiences and studies since Terry's death has to be that we all invent our own lives and, subsequently, our own death, difficult as it may be to grasp. After any of life's storms, this knowledge is the pot of gold at the end of the rainbow.

We choose our lives before we are born. We are not at the whim of fate at all. Our lives are in our own hands to mold, with our energy, as we see fit. It's God's greatest gift to us. An artist has his paints and the canvas to paint on. It's up to him to paint the picture he desires. With the artist, it's the paint and canvas. With us, our lives are the blank canvas, and our thoughts, feelings, and beliefs are the paint and paintbrushes we use to have what we call our lives.

If Terry knew consciously she came here in this lifetime and chose to be murdered as one of her life track choices, this story would never have been written or lived out. What lessons did she wish to learn by dying this way? And what lessons have I learned being the mother of a murdered child? Consciously, would I have chosen this? Hell no! But subconsciously, on a soul level, I certainly made this choice, and as I said before, now I know why I was part of this plan: to get this knowledge out to you. This is my passionate desire. If I don't, then all the carefully laid out plans become fruitless, and I won't accept that. Never.

Shortly after an Inventing Your Life workshop, I was chatting with a friend when it happened. I don't remember the exact date, but I will never forget that magic moment in time when I realized I finally got this. Terry's death was not what it seemed at all but part of a magnificent plan that caused my whole world and belief system to shake and shift. My beautiful daughter was not a victim as I had thought. This was all part of her own careful plan, something chosen by her on a soul or spirit level. It was at this time that Terry ceased being a victim and became the victor, and I ceased being a victim of loss and instead became the mother of an angel.

We come into this life with a plan, all of us. At some point, we need to commend ourselves for the courage it took to follow this plan we have no conscious memory of. By following my own plan, my own life track, it became crystal clear. I was to find this extraordinary gift and share it with as many as possible. This is the ultimate reason I shared my story and as every life has its purpose, sharing this knowledge with you, I know is mine. I invite you to accept this gift and am certain it will change your life for the better and ease whatever pain you are experiencing as it has mine. When you accept this gift, you can thank my teacher, Master Rose Ashley. Terry's death led me to her and her teachings. I will be forever indebted to them both because who I am today reflects all I learned at the monastery, and through all the classes I have been given. I am a part of it as it shall always be a part of me.

The death of a loved one begins many new journeys for those left behind. Terry's death set my feet onto a new path, away from the beliefs of my childhood, a path with breathtaking new possibilities. It reminds me of the words of Hafez, a mystic poet of 14th century Persia (Iran): "God, long ago drew a circle in the sand exactly around the spot where you are standing right now. You were never not coming here." I pray the death of your loved one leads you to the love and knowledge it led me to as you digest my own experiences. This is the purpose of sharing my story. We chose to be here in this lifetime. When we have completed and learned what we came here to learn and to experience, whether we are one year old or one hundred, we go home, and it's a huge celebration when we arrive! There may be tears here, but there will be cheers of joy, "there."

My journey began as a happily married woman with a wonderful husband and a daughter I loved with all my heart and soul. I was as ordinary as anyone else and thankful for all that God had given me. As I write this many years later, flooded with happiness, my life has come full circle and within that circle, Terry remains an intrinsic part and always will. I would be incomplete without her. Terry had the courage to play her part in the role she had chosen, and I had the strength to co-star.

How am I different from when I started my journey after my daughters' death is not as important to me as how different you will be as you begin your own journey. Your first step is to realize you are on a journey, a sacred one called your "life," keeping in mind you are a soul with a physical body wrapped around it to experience this life.

CHAPTER TWENTY

Maybe I had to experience all of this myself to finally understand where I really want this book, this story of my experiences, to lead the readers. Oh, it was all the things I have already written about, but until I experienced the conscious awareness of who we all are, how could I include it in this book? Now I can.

How many times have you heard the words, "We are all one." They are words, just words, forming a thought, a belief. They are very lovely words, all strung together like pearls of wisdom, and many espouse to agree wholeheartedly with them. But have you taken the time to examine the true meaning of these lovely words? Saying them reverently, or in a way that hinted I grasped their meaning, is perhaps what I was guilty of. I believed them. I accepted the concept. Then something happened. I experienced the "words" and now can't find the words to explain them: "We are all one."

How do you describe the air you breathe, a thought, the feeling of a magnificent sunrise or sunset? It is indeed an "Oh my God moment!"

These words draw you to God, the source of the words, and everything in creation. This is the God, the God of love we were born of and to. This is the love that sustains us at all times, a love that has no limits because God is limitless. This source's love is so great; it shared itself and became part of us as we became part of it, to share every breath of our life's experiences. We are all conscious beings, but everything is consciousness. Everything you lay eyes on has a consciousness, an awareness, not all at the same level, but consciousness is shared by everything. Everything is a part of this one consciousness that we call God. We are all pieces of God, be it a human being, a tree, the family dog, etc. "We are all one" are simple words. Their power is almighty. To become part of something is to be absorbed by it, becoming one with it. We, too, then, are God. Was that not what Christ told us centuries ago in so many words, words at that time, not understood? Was that not his purpose? Was Jesus not a gift from God to be the way-shower, an example of all we can be? Think about it.

Understanding we are one is a huge accomplishment because in understanding we are all one, we finally grasp the truth that we, each of us, are God, and in being God, have the ability, the power to have what we want in our lives. We are like a sun-struck drop of water shimmering in the light, encapsulating all our needs, dependent on no one but ourselves. Within this capsule of water is our world and this world is ours as we are its.

With each of us being pieces of one whole (God), it makes sense that we then must reflect each other in some way, as a broken mirror reflects each shard. If the reflection doesn't please you, does it mean it's not a true reflection of your own perception of yourself or does the reflection simply give you a picture of some way you might unknowingly be, not the exact reflection of whom you disapprove? If we are all part of each other, then there is a little of everyone in us and us in them. How can you hate someone else without hating a part of yourself? You can't.

So here we all are. Some people believe we're here to be one thing or another, and that's true to some extent. All are born for their own personal reasons, but within the big picture, we come to know that this is just a tiny part of why we are here, why we were born in the first place. The big picture is a true masterpiece, and with every stroke of the brush of time, laden with life's colorful experiences, it nears its completion. The completion is truly breathtaking; the end of the rainbow, labeled "your life," leads to the real reason for your existence.

For years you looked into a mirror and saw only what your mind wanted you or allowed you to see, based on its own fears and beliefs. Look into a mirror now and see the face of God reflected back. Introduce yourself to your real self.

You are the God of your own universe and the thing you call your life, which is a precious gift in itself. God (love) so loved us He divided himself into all that exists so everything would be a part of Him, an edict made at the beginning of time. You cannot move away from who you truly are, only by who you think you may be.

God's love is always engulfing you in its arms, but if you have never allowed yourself the gift of awareness, it seems the love is not there. Awareness is key!

This awareness is the gift lying within us all, patiently waiting to be discovered, and once found, ignites the fire in our soul, brilliantly radiating outward like a healing beacon to all humanity. This awareness leads you to God, something like the beginning of a lovely song wending its way to a magnificent crescendo, the climax of realizing what life is all about, all that is. Love. It is one love that defies description. Something comparable is the love a mother has for her child, but far surpassing it, and no matter who you are, no matter what you have done, be it good or bad in the eyes of humanity, you are loved beyond earthly measure. Not being aware of this love is life's biggest loss, not death itself.

The feeling of aloneness in today's world, spiked by negativity, is not due to lack of love but something sadder than that, the lack of awareness of the love that already exists. You can never be alone. You can feel alone, that may be your choice, but you can never be alone because you are a part of something greater than yourself, and that part is God itself. No matter what you think, do or say, will change this fact. It's not God's love you're seeking at all but the awareness of it.

Realizing the God-consciousness within and experiencing it is a surrender. It is the end of a battle, a truce when you admit who you are and at the same time wonder why you fought so hard to deny it, an acceptance of all you are and all you were given. At last, finally, there is peace. This battle with your mind is over, and new life and challenges begin. The challenge is coping with the truth of who you are and keeping your thoughts close in tow as you live moment to moment in this truth. No more pointing fingers and blaming others; gone are all those days, only acceptance of what you brought into your life for your own reasons and dealing with it, with the knowledge given to you. Pretty incredible, I think. For me, it brings immense gratitude at first, then the responsibility of owning your own life, and that is where the challenge floods in. Maybe we shouldn't call it a "flood," but let's call it a steady flow.

Challenges can be a nightmare or a call to action that is exciting. My choice is the call to action that brings excitement. All of my being is in step with this—even my mind is willing to bend to my soul's desires, and that's pretty awesome. Of course, it wants its time in the sun too, and I promised I would listen to what its concerns are, and we'll go from there.

Our journey begins with love and ends with love. What occurs between love and love are the life experiences you chose to fill the gaps with and grow. And these experiences are not all written in stone; you have choices, but your main reason for coming onto the stage of life was to play a specific role filled with lessons to learn. And yes, there is a God that hears our every prayer, and yes, you do have angels and guides on the other side that are actually there just for you. Answers do come out of the blue. My prayer is that as you read my story, new knowledge, light, and awareness enters, your heart opens, and bathed in this new light, begins to sing.

I know with a certainty when the curtain goes down on my life, Terry and I will joyfully be together once more, and hand in hand, smiling at each other, we'll take our final bows to the audience we called our "life."

Did Anyone Remember?

Did someone place a flower on her grave?
Did anyone remember her at all?
Miles away I find myself wondering
Flying to her side, if only in my mind.
Surely a single flower rests there.
Surely someone remembered.
I did.

A Rosary of Mothers' Tears

We stand apart from the others,
And in our "apartness", form an army
Reaching round the globe.
Not able to hold each other's hands,
We hold each other's hearts
With a newborn's fragility.
Can we survive the loss of our child?
No! Never!
But we do,
And in surviving, know our strength
Is from God and in
The rosary of tears
We have shed.

Mothers of Angels

When you don the mantle of motherhood, your child may bring you pain, joy, or a combination of the two. When you are blessed with a child that only brings you joy, you quickly realize that God has not entrusted you with a child but a special angel.

When you hold your child for the first time, it feels as if your heart left your body and entered that of your child. From that point forward, you feel whatever they feel. If they are in pain, so are you and the only way you can ease your pain is to ease theirs. It seems your very life depends on keeping your child safe and happy.

Your child becomes the center of your universe - your reason for being.

You might have a mate, friends, family, career, hobbies, and other things that occupy your time and mind, but your heart belongs to your child. You love as you never have before. You develop a fierceness you never knew you were capable of. Your heart expands beyond anything you believe possible. You are more than you ever were.

The worst thing that can happen to a mother is to lose her child. Her heart feels displaced because it can no longer dwell within her child. The mother doesn't want it to return to her body because she feels it belongs to her child, so she holds her heart at bay and lives as an empty shell. Eventually, this becomes too exhausting to maintain, so she allows her heart to return fully, and when it does, she doesn't recognize it. It is a pale shadow of what it used to be when it was colored by the love of her child.

The mother feels that her life will never be the same. It seems as if her heart will never recover. She puts one foot in front of the other but does not move forward. Instead, she circles in place, lost in a wilderness of emotion, searching and yearning for her child. She fears that if she leaves the space she occupies, her child might feel abandoned by her.

Eventually, the mother will accept that her child is not returning. She will begin to look up and around. Her loss is devastating, yet here she is, still alive. She wonders why. Is this some type of cruel punishment?

People will say to her, "Your child is with God. Your child is in a better place." But how can there be a place better for her child than within the embrace of her loving arms?

In time, the mother realizes that the only way her life can become bearable again is if she finds a new purpose, but she cannot imagine a higher purpose than holding her child's precious hand and surrounding her child with love. So, she seeks a lesser purpose to fill her days and ease her pain. Initially, she goes through the motions. Her body smiles and laughs at all the correct times, but her heart does not feel joy. What it feels is a terrible aching pain. The mother thinks the pain is coming from her loss, and all she can do is bear it, but the pain is not due to the loss.

The heart is designed to receive God's love, benefit from it then channel it to others. If we try to retain even a small part of that love, it becomes too painful for the heart to bear. A grieving mother accustomed to channeling God's love to her child may attempt to hold onto the love, keeping it in reserve for her child. This only serves to increase her pain. Relief will only come when she channels all of God's love to others.

Wake me up at 10:00, Love Terry is the story of one mother's journey from circling in place in the wilderness to discovering a new purpose. Fran's desire to heal her own pain led her to a desire to heal others. Whenever she saw a mother grieving over the loss of a child, she did not take comfort in the fact that someone else had lost a child. Instead, Fran's heart ached. She longed to heal grieving mothers and guide them to a place of hope and joy. Her desire initiated a spiritual journey which began with the realization that she needed to heal herself before she could heal others.

Fran's quest and new purpose returned her to a place of hope and joy. Today she serves as a living example of one mother who learned to fully channel God's love to others through her smile, humor, and unique words of comfort.

Master Rose Ashley

A portion of the sale of this book support the horses of Swan Center Outreach, a Spiritually based, non-profit sanctuary in California. Donations are tax deductible and always appreciated.

Printed in the United States
by Baker & Taylor Publisher Services